THE CHOICE FOR BETTER PARENTING

BETTER PARENTS

GREAT CHILDREN

HAPPIER FAMILIES

Robert Shimizu, M.D.

DEDICATION

For Judy

CONTENTS

DEDICATION iii

ACKNOWLEDGMENTS vii

PREFACE...1

CHAPTER 1: WHY PARENTING PRACTICES HAVE BEEN SO SLOW TO EVOLVE 5

CHAPTER 2: CHOOSING HOW TO PARENT – COMMITTING TO A BETTER PATH 11

CHAPTER 3: PARENTING 101 AND PARENTING 201 14

CHAPTER 4: THE PROBLEM WITH PARENTING 101 23

CHAPTER 5: SELF-ESTEEM - THE KEY.......................................33

CHAPTER 6: FINDING A NEW STARTING POINT 38

CHAPTER 7: KEY KNOWLEDGE - UNDERSTANDING BEHAVIORAL DEVELOPMENT 44

CHAPTER 8: FACTORS CONFUSING THE UNDERSTANDING OF BEHAVIORAL STAGES 48

CHAPTER 9: THE PROACTIVE PARENT.....................................61

CHAPTER 10: MENTORING AND TEACHING...............................70

CHAPTER 11: "BUT" 78

CHAPTER 12: SIBLING RELATIONSHIPS 86

CHAPTER 13: THINKING OUTSIDE OF THE BOX...........................98

CHAPTER 14: WHY THREATS AND PUNISHMENT DO NOT WORK 104

CHAPTER 15: ANOTHER LOOK AT COMPLIANCE, RESPECT, AND OTHER VIRTUES 110

CHAPTER 16: TEACHING GOOD BEHAVIOR, NOT JUST SETTING LIMITS 119

CHAPTER 17: FOSTERING RESPONSIBILITY, NOT DEMANDING IT.........128

EPILOGUE..136

APPENDIX: SPECIAL CASES...142

RECOMMENDED READING 152

ACKNOWLEDGMENTS

This book could not have been written without all of the wisdom and experience that my patients and their parents shared with me. Many insights came from our talks about raising their children. My growth as a pediatrician accelerated with learning to listen to what my parents had to say.

My family has been a wonderful resource, starting with my mother, who was ahead of her times in her kind, thoughtful approach to raising my brother and me. My wife, Judy, partnered with me in raising our children and helped me to understand our children's points of view and needs. My children, Daniel, Jenny, and Susie, were the ultimate guinea pigs who gave me instant feedback on how I was parenting. Charlie Rowe, M.D., started me writing with his encouragement and good ideas. Celine Shimizu, a college professor and my daughter-in-law, was my muse and main pusher along with her husband, my son, Daniel. Special thanks to Susie Williams, Sabrina Bea, and Tammy Kubalik for reviewing the book and for their suggestions.

The turning point book for me was Nancy Samalin's "Loving Your Child Is Not Enough, Positive Discipline That Works". It convinced me that a kinder, gentler style of parenting could work and result in a great child and a great parent-child relationship. I handed out many copies to my parents. When I started to write this book, it was the guiding spirit.

PREFACE

Before you were conceived I wanted you
Before you were born I loved you
Before you were here for an hour I would die for
you
This is the miracle of life

- Maureen Hawkins
  The Miracle

My thirty-nine year pediatric practice was in Lafayette, California, a bedroom community for many people who worked in Oakland and San Francisco. The practice was structured in a way that allowed us to spend more time with each patient than the usual busy suburban practice. At first, it seemed to be too much time for someone like me, inexperienced and limited in overall knowledge. I felt obliged to fill the time allotted to the family, so once I had run out of discussion about the physical health of the child, I started to ask about school and extracurricular activities and how the children got along. Subjects that we had not been trained to discuss, much less give advice.

It was like hitting a hidden water pipe while digging in your backyard. Everything came gushing out. Soon, these topics dominated these well-child visits, rather than the health issues. As you might expect, most of the children were physically quite healthy.

I was still interested and stimulated by interesting medical diagnoses, and taught residents at the Children's Hospital in Oakland for 30 years, but, I soon realized that I did not want any of my patients to have these "interesting diseases." I wanted them to grow and thrive and become healthy, happy, productive people. What I also began to realize was that daily dysfunction in the family caused more disruption and pain than most illnesses and never seemed to end.

What had started as a need to fill a full half hour visit began to be my favorite part of my practice. Often I would send the children out to the waiting room while the parents and I discussed how they were raising their child and why there were conflicts. Some of the time, I had ready advice for the parent, but at other times, we would talk out the situation together.

The latter were the better sessions for me because I learned from the practical experience of these parents. Their feedback of their good results made me reconsider what I had thought was good advice. It made the advice I gave to succeeding parents more relevant, tested, practical, and nuanced. Learning to listen to the parents helped me in all aspects of my practice and my family life. My wife and I, at this point, had not shaken off all of the confrontational aspects of Parenting 101.

I have read many books and articles over the years, and their ideas and theories helped me understand many areas of parenting better. But many of these books and articles seemed to miss the practicalities of daily living that these discussions brought out. These ideas began to have real meaning for me and my parents with our discussions about becoming a better parent and becoming positioned to raise a better child. It brought reality to the theories and ideas that were presented and helped to fill in or emphasize what seemed to be missing in the books.

We talked and discussed why, with all of their good intentions and love for their children, they still had angry exchanges and repeated problems. We examined all the layers of customs and practices and emotional issues that were hindering their understanding of the core issue - the establishing of a great parent-child relationship that preserved and nurtured the child's self-esteem. It became more apparent that if preserving the child's self-esteem was not underlying the parenting process, all of the good intentions and goals were not going to be fully met.

It took time for me to change my own point of view, but after I understood that the child's self-esteem was the key issue, it became clear that parents have the responsibility to model, mentor, and teach their child in a friendly way so that self-esteem was preserved and nurtured. The point was not just to prevent problems and bad behavior, it was more important to give children the tools and skills to succeed and become good and productive people. What was equally important was to create an atmosphere that was not contentious and off-putting. Parents can learn to open doors for their children, not just close them.

Remember, a positive relationship between the parent and child is the essential ingredient for successful parenting. It preserves your child's self-esteem and puts your child on a path to a happy productive life. The anger generated by an unhappy relationship makes it very difficult for the child to accept and learn important lessons. Raising a great child is a difficult challenge and requires a lot of work and giving on the part of the parent. All the more reason that you and your child should enjoy the process and reap the rewards that come from a positive happy relationship during this epic life journey you are taking together.

CHAPTER 1: WHY PARENTING PRACTICES HAVE BEEN SO SLOW TO EVOLVE

Parenting has always been complicated, full of joy and love and wonderful moments, and at the same time, disappointments, anger, and confrontations.

After so many generations of parenting, why haven't we gotten it down more perfectly? Shouldn't it be mostly enjoyable and without major conflict and unresolved issues? Shouldn't parents have tweaked and corrected most of the problems by now?

In the high tech world, products have steadily and consistently have had their glitches uncovered, corrected and perfected. In the workplace a good and thoughtful boss takes positive and proactive steps to root out conflicts and aims to make the environment work well for everyone. Why has this model of solving and correcting problems gone so slowly with parents and their children?

Problems with an imperfect product are studied from all sides, no part is considered above scrutiny. No part is okay just because it has always been there, and thus above criticism and needs no further assessment. Engineers would not take this approach and they would reassess every part of a malfunctioning product, no matter how long it has been a part of the product.

In the work setting, problem people are pulled aside and interviewed and consulted on better ways of interacting with subordinates and peers. New strategies and points of view are discussed.

In parenting the opposite has been true. The Principles of Parenting seem to be engraved in stone, and not easily challenged, much less changed. The role of the parents and the parenting positions brought to their relationship with their child have not been critically examined and even are held above question. But, how much does the average parent know about the theory of being in charge of teaching another person how to conduct themselves, what works, what doesn't? The goals of Parenting 101 are generally reasonable, but, the methods of Parenting101 have proven over the years to still engender a lot of family discord and anger.

There has been little serious discussion of the parent's lack of experience or knowledge as a major factor in the "natural conflicts that occur in every family." Over the years parents/adults have put in clichés about children being "naturally stubborn, willful, disobedient, and rebellious at certain times in their lives (the terrible twos and the teenage rebellion are the classics) to explain ongoing problems. This allows the parents to blame the discord on the children (and nature), and the children are in no position to effectively fight or point their finger back at their parent. It also is the cardinal rule of traditional parenting; not questioning "Parental Authority".

Brainstorming sessions between the parents and the grandparents rarely occur. Does a new parent really want to relive the conflict that they experienced and resented as a child? The mistakes and conflicts that aggravated their relationship are difficult to discuss, probably because some of the issues are still unresolved and festering. Also, the goals and methods of raising a child are not always agreed upon by the parents and grandparents. It is hard for the grandparent to admit that they were wrong in their principles and methods.

Do we not reflect on the process because we only have one shot at it? One and done. Then we reminisce about the problems we had with half a smile but no need to consider changing tactics to make the next time better. There isn't a next time. No need to reflect on why our children were so sullen and uncommunicative at times. It was just the age, "not anything that could be corrected. I couldn't make him talk." But, perhaps you could have changed the atmosphere so that he would feel less intimidated and resentful and freer to talk. Then he might feel that you were actually willing to listen to what he had to say and feel free to give his point of view.

The disproportionate balance of power allows the parent to treat their child's protests with distain and even anger for challenging their authority. No one feels comfortable criticizing other parents (and thus themselves). Further, society puts them on the defensive if they seem too easy and soft on their children. An axiom of parenting was that you couldn't be a friend to your child and be an effective patent. Implying that you had to be harsh and threatening at times to effectively get your points across to your undisciplined child.

The point of this book is that while we are becoming better parents over the generations, it is at too slow a pace. We have been too willing to accept conflict as an unfortunate side effect of being a strong parent. We have not critically looked at our role as the parent and what drives us to accept the traditional stances that lead to so much discord in the parenting process. It is hard to change generations of beliefs and practices.

We Should Be Our Child's Best Friend!

In fact, we must be!

The difference between doing the right thing and just being obedient and compliant

W. Edwards Deming, management consultant, might say that if you have to yell at and threaten someone to get the job done, you have made a mistake and hired the wrong person for the job. In a parent's case, they must learn to deal with the child before them. It is not the child's duty to handle every situation that their parent has presented to them, it is the parent's job to put their child in situations that are within their capabilities. It's not the child, it's the situation. The conflict is a product of putting the child in a situation that is beyond their behavioral maturation.

How do you know that he is not purposefully opposing you or testing you? Because your child wants nothing more than to have you be happy with and approve of him. A two or three year old can't do what you are asking him to do exactly as you want him to, because his behavioral maturation cannot meet the task asked of him. He may cooperate under duress, but not because he understands, but because he is fearful of the anger and rejection of his parent. Aiming anger and shame at him, and threatening him does not make him understand better what needs to be done and why. These early conflicts often begin a pattern of unreasonable demands and confrontations.

Obedience and compliance are traits that a parent

wants in their child. While theoretically, the parent may have wanted their child to have these traits for lofty reasons, in the end they are sometimes simply sought as a sign of submission to the authority of the parent. When the child asks why he must do something, the frustrated parent not having a good response, will angrily say, "because I'm your parent and I said so!" No logic or reasoning why it is good to be cooperative and helpful in the family.

In the long run, compliance and obedience are rarely sustained as a result of threats. What is missing is a reasonable explanation for the order and an amicable resolution. Do we want our child to just bow to authority or do we want him to understand what is right or at least a better way to do something? The fly in the ointment is that we lose sight of the key factor, the child's maturity level. The perceived importance of the lesson being taught often overrides the fact that the child is too immature to learn and to comply in the way demand of him.

It is difficult to escape the past and to change practices that seemed to have on the whole worked in the end. This is especially true in families that had their share of conflicts, but overall seem to get along after the children have grown up. "After all, every family has its problems, it's only natural" is the rationale. But, not all families emerge unscathed. There can be long-lasting resentments and conflicts. I have had parents tell me that they rarely interact with their parents or siblings because of contentious experiences when they were growing up. Even those who feel okay (not great) about their upbringing still have a few issues that carry into adulthood.

If the child just complies in order to avoid punishments that he has experienced in the past, has he really learned how to do the right thing and for the right reasons? It's better to continue to teach and mentor and model until it becomes clear that he understands what works best for him and his family in a given situation. This is a key insight for the parent, that their child is not stubborn, but is immature and actually developmentally unable to always comply perfectly.

Compliance and obedience to the parent's satisfaction are not the end points of parental guidance. The child becoming mature enough to understand the problem and learn how to handle the situation for the right reasons is the true end point of parenting.

The other major negative for the child in these conflicts is the loss of self-esteem. The use of anger, belittling, disappointment, and threats are methods that all attack our children's feelings about themselves. We want to teach our children to make the right choices for the right reasons, not because they fear anger or loss of love from their parents. These negative techniques coming from the one that they most want to love and value them is devastating to their self-esteem.

Removing anger, tension, and belittling from the family dynamics is the biggest benefit of this approach. How great it is to feel and know that your parents are happy with you and appreciate you. The child is unaware that you are patient and thoughtful in the beginning, but as they mature they see and appreciate your thoughtfulness and positive care of them. You have enabled them to meet the world with confidence and instilled resilience in them.

CHAPTER 2: CHOOSING HOW TO PARENT – COMMITTING TO A BETTER PATH

What Is Your Idea of a Dream Parent?

If you could go back in time and construct the perfect parent for yourself, what would be the most important traits?

- Loving
- Understanding
- Willing to listen to me
- Helps me to reach my goals, but lets me try on my own
- Sets strong guidelines for behavior and shows me how to reach them

The things that you don't want to hear coming from your parent (or later from your boss).

- Angry and derogatory words

- Words that shame or belittle you
- Being compared unfavorably to someone else
- Demanding and threatening (not teaching) to get better behavior
- Withdrawal of love or approval when the demands are not met

While most parents would pick the friendlier, more positive approach, they still have some reservations about being too easy-going about problems with their child.

Fears of the "Good Parent"

Becoming an enabler or pushover is a great fear of parents. How much help and prodding is too much? The hovering and over controlling parent has always been an issue, but has become more so with the increase in competition for college admittance and jobs. The "soccer Mom" has been replaced by the "helicopter Mom" as the label of an overbearing, unapologetic mother of the times.

The pressure of increased completion has pushed the feeling that while "we don't want to be so involved, the times demand it". The problem is that the parent (mom or dad) feels the pressure and expects too much too soon from their child and reacts in a negative way because "they are not trying or working hard enough". Instead of helping their child to do well, they often are only demanding they do better. How does anger and shaming help the child move forward?

Since parents of this generation have been taught to forego corporeal punishments, the tactics to demand results have become more indirect and seemingly more subtle. The parent feels justified that they are "being tough for their child's good", but the child does not feel the disappointment and shaming is subtle. It reaches the core of their self-esteem. Feeling that they have loss the love and approval of their parent is devastating.

Some parents feel that a harsh lesson turned them around and it may have, but, I think that it worked out positively because there was a reasonable relationship in place before the incident. The parent and child had many positive interactions with their own parents or authority figure before the harsh lesson. Still, a better path could have been taken.

In this book we will discuss the traditions, jargon and attitudes that have hindered parents from finding this better path that mentors and teaches and guides our children and preserves their self-esteem.

CHAPTER 3: PARENTING 101 AND PARENTING 201

What Principles Guide Your Parenting Techniques?

When we buy something expensive we consider many factors, cost, need, and specific features of the product. For a house or a new car there is a lot of research and give and take. "No, I think a convertible won't work with our third on the way!" Usually there is a more serious discussion before the decision of how to proceed is made.

With parenting, why is less thought given? Is there anything more important to you and your children than how you choose to raise them? Do we actually stop and discuss what methods we will use to raise our children?

First of all we are overwhelmed with the whole idea of our first baby. Getting feedings established, getting sleep for the baby and you, and finding time to do everything else becomes a survival drill. Most parents have read how to do these tasks during the pregnancy and they soon become manageably and routine. Parents can feel that this wasn't so bad and enjoy the whole experience of their beautiful and amazing baby more and more.

Are you being led down the "garden path"? Yes, you are. It is wonderful and gets easier for the first eight or nine months or so. Then the big change occurs, the child becomes mobile! Efforts to control the child's mobility begins, and so controlling behavior becomes a major issue. The problem is that the process slowly slides in and parents are not totally aware that a new era with their child has begun. There should be a big sign that says, "Your child is mobile, everything is going to change!"

Without consciously realizing it, the parent's job description now includes teaching and enforcing the rules of conduct. There is not only a demand by tradition for the parent to become a disciplinarian, there is also an implied threat that the lax parent will end up with an out of control toddler and teenager.

Often at this point, less preparatory study about parenting is done because parents are so busy in their everyday routines and are getting immediate off the cuff advice from family and friends. The path taken is often an immediate reaction to a problem, rather than proactively preparing ahead. Tradition, spoken and unspoken, has told new parents that there is a way to raise children. It is what I call Parenting 101, rules and regulations that have been passed from generation to generation.

These are some of its features.

Parenting 101

- The parent is unquestionably in charge.
- The child must obey all orders from the parent.

- Punishment maybe needed to force stubborn children to obey.
- If these tactics don't work, you must not give in, and use harsher punishments if necessary.
- An adversarial relationship is sometimes an unfortunate result of maintaining discipline.

Instead of just accepting these traditional rules, look at the possibility of another approach. Take the time to consciously and deliberately consider whether it is possible to raise the kind of child you envision in a friendlier and less confrontational way. From the following lists, choose either A or B.

- Parent's role
  - o A. Disciplinarian/authoritarian
    - Traditional parenting (Parenting 101) is based on maintaining discipline by strict enforcement of rules. It can become adversarial as the parent resorts to threats and punishments to demand obedience and get compliance. Bad behavior is limited by threat of punishment.
  - o B. Teacher/mentor
    - The alternative is modelling, mentoring, and teaching. Unacceptable behavior is stopped quickly, but in a friendly nonthreatening way. The child's behavioral developmental stage is referenced and parental action is adapted to the child's abilities.
- Child

- o A. Seen as stubborn and non-compliant
    - Traditional opinions tell parents that their child will be naturally disobedient and stubborn and will need to be disciplined to stop bad behavior and get compliance. Disciplinary steps are often started before two years of age.
- o B. Seen as innocent and immature
    - Viewing the child as innocent and immature leads the parent to consider whether the child is really capable of doing what is asked of them. Repeated failures lead the parent to consider whether a seemingly simple situation is too difficult for the child and should be handled cooperatively until his maturity catches up.
- Atmosphere
    - o A. Stern, serious interventions
        - When rules are broken and orders not carried out, the parent should show their disappointment and anger for the child's failure and think of a suitable punishment that will make them remember the lesson. The unacceptability of their conduct should be emphasized so that it will not be repeated in the future. Being a friend to your child is not compatible with being a strong parent.
    - o B. Friendly, helpful interventions
        - Promptly stop the problem and teach a better way, there is no need to shame

her or to be overly stern. Remember she is immature and needs your help and guidance, not angry demands. Do not threaten or denigrate her.

- Responsibility In Reaching Parenting Goals –
  - o A. Demanding obedience and compliance
    - In traditional parenting (Parenting 101), obeying and complying can become more important to the parent than the completion of the task. Disappointment in the child is often shown. Penalties are threatened and demands made of children to reach goals.
  - o B. Parental leadership in teaching how to reach goals
    - The parent is the one who is mature enough to change and solve impasses in a mutually acceptable way. When preserving the child's self-esteem is always considered as the lessons are taught, not only will the child learn the right course, he will feel valued by his parents and confident in his ability to handle similar situations in the future. He will be willing to tackle difficult problems and even if he fails to reach his goal, he will have the resilience to try again.

The second choices take a more positive, proactive, and cooperative approach to parenting. They are the basis for Parenting 201. Isn't it logical that the adult whose IQ is at least 3X greater than the child, not only be in charge, but just as important, be responsible for making the child-parent relationship work in a friendly and still productive way.

Parenting 201

- The parent is the leader of the family but also understands and considers their child's developmental stage, feelings, and point of view.
- The child's behavioral maturity needs to be clearly understood.
- Inappropriate behavior is quickly and firmly stopped without harshness or shaming.
- The parent is the one wise and mature enough to find solutions for conflicts
- Modelling, mentoring, and teaching of good behavior take the place of demands and threats of punishments.
- Interventions are neutral or friendly in nature and, more importantly, keep in mind the child's self-esteem and foster trust in the child.

The main difference between Parenting 101 and Parenting 201 is how you are trying to educate and advance your children. Parenting 101 tries to create better behavior by making demands on the children with threat of consequences. Parenting 201 takes in to account the child's maturation and changes the parent's point of view and encourages a better model, teacher and mentor for their children.

Early in my career, it was common practice for some

child psychologists to spend the majority of their time talking to their patient, the child. Little time was spent with the parents, and some parents related that they were not informed about what was being discussed on the grounds of patient confidentiality. It did not seem logical to me that the child whether 5 or 15 was the one that should be educated to make a bad situation work. It made more sense that teaching the parents to understand better and friendlier ways to interact with their children would be far more effective. The psychologist and the parents acted as if the parent already knew how to do the right thing, and only the child needed to change.

But, is a child mature enough to change the situation, when the parent is not changing any of their methods or attitudes? It made more sense that convincing the parent to choose a more child aware and friendly parenting path, even without a psychologist teaching the child how to deal with a misguided parent. First, change the harsh and adversarial approach of the parent. If the parent has learned a thoughtful and proactive positive way to raise their child, there is no need to teach the child how to cope with their parents. Having chosen Parenting 201, the parent and child embark on a journey of mentor and student, with the older and wiser teaching and guiding the younger and less mature how to navigate life.

Commit to finding this parenting style that preserves, enhances, and values the child's self-esteem and aims for a lifelong great parent-child relationship. Really make a commitment. It's harder to do than you would think, and many early attempts to change your methods won't automatically change your child's behavior. It's all too common for parents to become frustrated when their early efforts at kinder methods fail. Simply being less harsh doesn't suddenly change everything. There are many traditional beliefs and clichés that must be reexamine for their validity and replaced with a new starting point that considers the child's immaturity, feelings, and point of view.

Consider whom parenting should benefit. Is it the child or the parent? Traditional parenting consciously or unconsciously was for the child to please the parent. Parents were consciously trying to raise their children to become good and productive adults, but unconsciously they were stressing compliance and obedience to the parent as the central goal. The need to have obedience was the rationale for being harsh at times and threatening punishments when demands were not met. It was the sine qua non of parenting 101.

Parenting 201 is for the child and the parent, with the parent reaping many rewards for learning to parent in a positive, proactive style. Understanding what your child is developmentally capable of doing allows the parent to know when to intervene and help the process along, instead of stubbornly insisting on compliance to their unmet orders. The child soon learns that they can always get help from their parent whenever they have a problem. The child learns that they can always trust their parent. The parent's love for the child is not obscured by harsh and shaming words

In the next chapter we will discuss in detail the issues that make it hard to shed the dictates of Parenting 101.

Things Parents Should Never do to Their Children

- Shame them
- Threaten them
- Act angry towards them

- Withdraw your love for them

These are traditional substitutes that parents use instead of learning how to teach, mentor, and model good behavior.

Better Parenting Choices

- Be clear on what your limits and rules are.
- Stop unacceptable behavior, promptly and firmly without recriminations: see above.
- Consider your child's behavioral development
  o Change the situation if your child seems to be too immature to handle the situation consistently.
  o Teach, model, and mentor if they are mature enough to understand and cooperate.
- You have the responsibility to find a good and mutually satisfying solution; it is not up to your child to comply just because you said so.
- Maintain a sense of humor; remember your children needs to know how much you love them.

CHAPTER 4: THE PROBLEM WITH PARENTING 101

All happy families are alike; each unhappy family is unhappy in its own way.

- Leo Tolstoy
  Anna Karenina

Family dysfunction is so painful.

- Martha Smith

They fuck you up, your mum and dad
They fill you with the faults they had
And add some extra, just for you

- Philip Larkin
  This Be the Verse

At the end of a physical examination, a mother and I

were discussing her son. I asked about his school work, and she responded with a big smile that he was doing great and was deciding between several great colleges. When I suggested that she must be very proud of him, she unexpectedly began to cry. They were obviously not tears of joy, and I asked what was wrong.

She said, "Everyone admires him and tells me how lucky I am to have such a fine son. "Other mothers never failed to rave about him and when he was younger, told her to send him over to play any time. Even in high school other parents and his teachers were all complimentary of him." So, why the tears?

"We just do not get along at all," she said. In fact, that very week she had seen him through the front window talking to an elderly couple across the street for whom he did yard work. They were all smiling and laughing. But, when he came into the house and saw his mother, the smile instantly changed to a scowl and he stormed into his room.

"He was very stubborn and always hard for me to handle. I had to use strong discipline to keep him in line when he was young. If I asked him to pick up his toys it would quickly become a power struggle ending in threatening him with consequences. I even spanked him once when he yelled back at me. I hated punishing him, but it was for his own good. I told him that it hurt me more than it hurt him to have to punish him, and I wished that he would listen the first time. As he got older he would do the minimum of any chore asked of him, and would hardly respond to me."

I have heard this scenario, with small variations on the theme, many times. It occurs in "good families", wanting nothing more than to have their children do well and succeed in life. The goals are good. The parents love their child and have great ambitions for them. They want them to be successful and happy. So what has gone wrong?

The Ends Do Not Justify the Means

Most of us have excellent goals and ideals for our children, but the hard part is reaching these ends with means acceptable not only to the parent but the child as well. Parenting 101 has taught parents to enforce limits and demand respect, obedience, and compliance. It justifies the use of threats and punishments as means to reach these goals. The conflict that results is seen as an unfortunate consequence of being a strong parent. But, stop and consider, why do we accept this line of thought?

In this story, we have a fairly typical loving family with good standards and a strong desire for their child to do well. Early in his life there were probably many confrontations over putting toys away and doing simple chores. The parents used coercion, threats, shows of disappointment, and anger to emphasis their frustration that their child was not obeying their orders. But, the child was too young and developmentally immature to understand the issues and to respond as his parents wanted him to respond. They were concentrating on the ends so much that they did not see the destructiveness of their means. Teaching the child to put away his toys or finish any chore was no longer the goal, the goal was getting obedience.

The child, as he grew older and became able to think abstractly, began to perceive and feel the hostility and disappointment that was directed at him when he did not comply. The parents' love and concern for him were obscured by their methods. While he resented their treatment of him, he learned to live within their rules, but the parent/child relationship gave neither of them much satisfaction.

Often the parent is too busy to spend enough time really discussing better ways for the child to handle the situation when it comes up.   Some busy parents only seem to have time for solutions for the moment. They just want to put a Band Aid on it and stop it for now and get back to their busy life.   The quick fix is only temporary, and the same issue keeps coming back up because the means have not changed.   Not only is it not being resolved, now it is becoming frustrating and infuriating to both the parent and the child that the problem keeps coming back.

The dictates of Parenting 101 have been accepted not only as traditional guidelines of parenting, but also seem to have become laws that the parent do not question. Repeated confrontations with our children should lead parents to consider different means.   Stopping to brainstorm the issues and methods with spouse or friend or seeking professional help is always helpful.

Letting Out Anger at Home

A common warning sign that traditional child-raising practices are too harsh is that you are not getting along with your child at the same time that your friends and your child's teachers can only say how great she is.

One friend, the mother of three, put it this way. "I feel like I raised six children; the three that I had to punish, fight, and scold to keep in line at home, and the (same) three that were praised by teachers and friends as being so wonderful."

Evidently she had gotten her points across, but at what cost?   Clearly, she was not benefiting from her efforts as much as other adults in her children's lives. The children at some level sees the wisdom or logic of her words and feel her love, but have been so turned off by the authoritarian tactics of Parenting 101 that they will not openly agree with what she has said. They will not give her full cooperation even when she has a valid point.

Another common expression of this is "the angry child who takes out all her frustrations from her school day out on her parents in the safety of her home." But, it is the same issue as in our first example. The child is probably being treated in a reasonable way at school, and in an arbitrary way at home. She is frustrated with her parents' methods (means) and is acting out because of their misguided tactics, not letting out anger from imagined problems at school.

For many parents it is hard to set strong limits and still do it in a kind manner because most of us have grown up with ideas about Parenting 101 that do not support this combination. Parenting 101 has instructed us to take a hard line when we have issues with our child, and demand that they change/comply rather than simply helping them to understand how to deal with the problem better. Unhappy relationships are too often the end result of these encounters.

Have strong principles and guidelines; learn to teach them in a child friendly way.

Detachment From the Family

There are varying degrees of detachment by children living under the rules of Parenting 101. One child may be totally alienated and run away from home or engage in behavior counter to all that the family stands for. Many children are like the boy in our story, who are upset and angry but still abide by the family's rules, although they show they are not happy about the way they are enforced. Others have accepted the conditions, and while they may not agree with the way the parents run their lives, they still go along with it and have a reasonably happy relationship with their parents.

These children are stereotyped by their parents as the black sheep, the feisty one who lets his anger out at home where it is safe, and the golden child. Underneath it all they have the same problem, they are not completely happy with the means used to raise them.

Parents point to their "golden child" as proof that they are good parents and that they are unlucky to have a "bad seed". They do not like the hostility they feel from their other children, but reluctantly accept it as an inevitable consequence of being a "strong" parent, not a pushover.

In the past and now, parents have taken credit for the good and denied the blame for the bad. The idea that children need to meet any and all demands of their parents is such a strong tenet of traditional parental beliefs that it prevents most parents from reconsidering their own role in the impasse. This state of affairs has come about because Parenting 101 has given all the power to the parents and expects them to use it. While it is certainly reasonable and desirable to have the parents in charge that does not mean that the children's interests should be ignored when there is a difference of opinion.

Children should be seen and heard.

Repeating History

My family and I were having dinner in a local restaurant, when we heard some chairs at the next table clatter to the hardwood floor. We looked up and saw a father hauling his four or five year old under his arm out the front door, not stopping to pick up the chairs he had knocked over. He was on a mission. The mother and grandmother and an older brother were still at the table. It was hard to tell whether they were embarrassed or approving, as the mother said in our direction, "Anyone want a little boy"? Shortly, we finished our meal and I looked at the little boy who was back seated at the end of the table.

He had the saddest face and tears in his eyes, and his head down on his arms, while everyone else was talking. It was so pathetic to see. This family out to enjoy themselves, and their time is interrupted by a harsh lesson put on their youngest in public for who knows what offense. Can't an adult think of a better solution to their child's disruptive actions. Would we even think of doing so harsh and demeaning to anyone else but our own child? Who has given permission to this father to act in such an abrasive and cruel way? I think that the one thing that is sure, the child will remember how his father made him feel, sad, defeated, and angry. And sadly, it is probably not the first time, nor will it be the last.

The father may protest that this, indeed, was not the first time this happened and that is why he acted so abruptly and harshly. But, the repetitiveness of the situation also indicates that these strong arm tactics have been used before and have not permanently solved the problem. It should be a signal to the father and mother to think of better ways to deal with their child's behavior.

Parents, who remember having had great conflicts with their parents, amazingly seem to follow the same techniques of Parenting 101 that their parents employed on them. When the parent had grown up and left home and gotten married and had his own children, if the conflicts were not too great, his own parents' harshness is forgotten and/or forgiven and their love and sacrifices become more prominent and clear. Now, as he has conflicts with his own children, he blames himself for being "bad" like his own children are now, and can "understand" why his parents had to be so harsh with him. The fact that the parents really cared about them does not change the fact that they used overly harsh methods that need to be changed.

And so the cycle of Parenting 101 continues.

Us-Against-Them

Hazing as a rite of passage continues to show its ugly head in news stories of students dying in the course of these events in fraternities, college bands, and team sports hazing. For archaic misguided reasons these rituals are carried on in the name of bonding. How is there heart-felt bonding for someone who abuses and demeans you? Is it because you will soon have your turn to abuse someone else?

In contrast, my grandson's high school wrestling team assigned the upper classmen to mentor the lower classmen. The lower classmen talked in glowing terms of their mentors, grateful for their advice and support and friendship. Bonding was very strong and positive, a good example for parenting. It is a positive rite of passage.

Unfortunately, for some, our parenting tradition has brought an us-against-them mentality in raising our child.

At my grandchildren's soccer games I have been asked for sympathy from parents about their problems with their teenagers. The tone is a woe-is-me, help me through this unavoidable nightmare, rather than what can they do to make their relationship work better.   I felt that sympathy was wanted more than advice, especially when I mentioned that they should consider changing their approach.

It is hard for many parents to fully embrace a kinder and gentler approach to their children when their own life experience, Parenting 101, was one of unquestioned parental authority, along with societal reproach for the "soft parent". In my day, these parents fell under the category of "hippie parents", parents who did not take charge of their children and allowed them to run wild and wreak havoc on the rest of us. While this stereotype was not really true, there seemed to be no middle ground for the parent. The impression was that either you were tough and ready to punish unacceptable behavior or you were too easy and your child would grow up without respect for others.

The ability of a parent to successfully impart life lessons to their child is directly related to the bond between them. Has there been so much anger in getting your point across that the child feels upset and unloved, even though you have expressed how much you love your child?   Your actions and attitude need to fit your words.

The cooperation that is gotten by coercive techniques lasts only as long as the child fears the consequences.

Look at it from a different perspective and think about how we react to a harsh, dictatorial teacher or boss. Can we get past the anger that they have generated and accept the advice being given? A good benchmark for parents is to consider whether or not your child is upset after an encounter. Are we sitting on the same side of the table, or are we sitting across from each other, glaring?

Do not accept the dictates of Parenting101 and take discord between you and your child as being an unavoidable consequence of being a "good tough" parent. Make sure she clearly and absolutely knows how much you love and want to help her after you have discussed a tough problem.

Goals of Parenting - Raising a Child:

- Who likes himself and has great self esteem
- Who can stand up to peer and societal pressures
- Who looks at life as an opportunity and wants to explore it
- Who is good and productive and makes a positive impact
- Who likes his parents and sees them as lifelong resources
- Who along with his parents enjoys the whole process

The Three Most Important Issues of Parenting

- Self Esteem
- Trust
- Love

CHAPTER 5: SELF-ESTEEM - THE KEY

Most discussions lead you down a path of information and discovery and save its important points and the punchline for the end. This is the path that I took as I thought and wrote about parenting. This book was started in a logical manner as I explored the problems of traditional parenting and then proposed a change in starting point and point of view. But, as I neared the end of putting my thoughts on paper, it became clear that the heart of successful parenting was about nurturing and maintaining your child's self-esteem and that this needed to be highlighted closer to the beginning of the book. As you parent, keep in mind that your child's self-esteem is the touchstone that you need to come back to, as you interact with and help him to become a good and productive adult.

At first, I didn't clearly see the child's self-esteem as being the central issue. The writing process helped me to realize how difficult it is to dig out from under traditional thinking and shine new light on a complex subject. The traditions of parenting are especially difficult to critically examine and change because we are so emotionally engulfed in them, first as a recipient and then as givers of the traditions and rules.

At the beginning of this process, my starting point was to help parents simply find a friendlier way to raise their child, so that both parties had a mutually enjoyable relationship. In discussing and thinking about the book I found that it was like peeling an onion. At first we were only looking at the outer layers of the problem.

As an example, with discipline, many were appalled with past heavy handed physical punishments, and switched to verbal threats, feeling they were doing better than their parents. But, the psychological impact was not too different in its negative effect on the child. The change to verbal punishment was a step in the right direction but was not the complete answer. More layers needed to be peeled away.

The next layer was to understand and eliminate the anger and alienation that was created by the punishment, whether physical or verbal. This process in turn needed to be taken another layer deeper. Parents needed to find a way to proactively teach good behavior, instead of just trying to find ways to limit bad behavior by threats and punishments. Finally, we were reaching the core, teaching and mentoring as the way to advance our children. It followed that consideration and preservation of the child's self-esteem is the reference point around which our parenting practices needed to revolve.

There are three elements to building your child's self-esteem. First, it needs to be protected from being torn down by negative encounters and words where shaming and disappointment are used to point out misbehavior. Simply and firmly stopping the behavior is enough. You can make your standards clear in a firm but nice way.

During a writing exercise class, the instructor had my

classmates circle me and yell out at me as a wayward child. "What is wrong with you, can't you even do one thing right?" "Your little brother could have done better!" "Why are you so lazy?" "No thanks, after all that we've done for you." "You keep screwing up no matter how nicely we ask"? And worse.

It was easy for me to smile at these words at first, but as they continued to circle and their tone became harsher and their fingers began stabbing towards me, I started to feel the anger in their voices and the anger rising in me. I was almost ready to jump up and yell, "shut up" at these kind fellow writers of mine.

It gave me a sense of what a child must feel when these angry scornful words are hurled at them. But, the child receives them in a real and defenseless way facing the person that they most want to love them.

Tradition dictates the choice of words must be harsh, disappointed, and demeaning when a child argues or does not comply or quickly obey. There is a sense that the worse the issue in the parent's eyes the more negative and angry the parental tone should be.

But, the child knows there is a problem as soon as he is stopped. Does degrading him and attacking his self-esteem help him learn his lesson better? Many parents will say that the problem was very important and needed special emphasis to make it a lesson that would not soon be forgotten. The reality is that the child probably remembers the harshness of the punishment and his parent's disappoint in him more than the lesson that was being taught.

It is more effective to simply and promptly stop the undesirable or inappropriate behavior in a calm way and then teach in a firm but friendly way what you want them to do. Repeated prompt, firm interventions will let your child know that the issue is important and make him more receptive to suggestions.

The second and third points are that parents still have to teach the right way to approach the problem and in a proactive helpful way. It is not enough to simply threaten more severe punishment if it happens again. If the atmosphere is hostile how much is actually listened to and learned. The child needs to feel that his parent is trying to help him deal with his problem for his benefit and with concern for his feelings.

If the child feels that his parents are always trying to help him in a firm, but friendly way, he will begin to understand that they are a good source to come to for guidance. The child will have trust in his parents. He will not feel a need to hide difficult situations, but instead feel comfortable seeking their help. He will become able to turn the respect that his parents give him into self-respect and confidence in himself. Now he will be able to handle his own encounters with life with confidence in what he (and his parents) believe is right.

It is imperative that parents learn how to proactively model, teach, and mentor their children in a friendly way. Negative words and encounters erode the self-esteem we want our children to have. It obscures our love for them and makes it hard for them to trust their parents in difficult situations. There is a way to reach your goals in a way that preserves all this, you need to persist and commit to finding it for you and your children.

The rewards are a lifelong loving relationship and a good, confident, and productive person.

Self-esteem, trust, and love are the gifts that keep giving. Each aspect depends and feeds on the others. If you have raised your children with concern for their self-esteem, they will know that they can trust you to be there for them because they know you love them so much. When they know you trust them, it bolsters their self-esteem and confirms your love for them. Really feeling that their parents love them is at the heart of everything.

You know how much you love and value your children, make sure your words and actions let them know this too.

CHAPTER 6: FINDING A NEW STARTING POINT

The Problems Start Here – Too Much Is Expected Too Soon

As parents take their roles with their children, how do they view them?   Children are accepted as being pretty perfect in the first one to two years.   At first it is a no-brainer, they are adorable and perfect, and there is nothing to do, but keep them safe and healthy and love them. They are seen as being innocent and their antics as cute, we can't wait to tell everyone how funny or clever they are. In our culture the behavioral issues of parenting begin around one and a half or two years when tradition tells parents to start expecting their child to respond appropriately to parental commands. The question is, on what basis is it decided that two is when the child should understand and obey all parental commands.

In fact, some parents begin their demands when the child becomes mobile at around nine months. Most parents see this as too early to expect total compliance, but seem to feel that they need to start this pattern of demands and threats of consequences because the child is now moving and "getting into trouble" on his own. One mother related to me that she did not go to grandma's house with her toddler because grandma refused to put anything breakable or dangerous away because the child needed to learn to behave by stern threats and consequences. Rather than child-proof the house until the child was more mature, grandma felt that harsh confrontations and punishments taught the lesson better.

Your attitude may come from grandparents and parents of older children who may hint or even loudly and exasperatingly complain how difficult children (you) were at two. When they break family rules tradition says your children need to be reprimanded and informed of their bad behavior and punished to teach them a lesson about not breaking the rules. "I hate to be so hard on him, but it's for his own good."

There is the fact that your child did a simple chore perfectly once or even twice. Seeing the child follow orders on one occasion can make some parents believe that their child should always do the same task in the future. There is also a traditional belief that the child is not immature, but stubborn at two and that the parent must overcome this now to avoid bigger problems from developing.

The fact that parents have always had an all-powerful position in this relationship has also made it difficult for the parent to consider changing rules of their own behavior.

Precedence for change of long held beliefs about the traditional superiority of one group over another has been challenged in recent years. Women and racial minorities have made many gains towards equality and understanding because they are able to argue their point and convince others that change was just and needed.

Unfortunately, children are not in a position to debate their issues with their parents. Young children are not able to rebut their treatment because the toddler and pre-teen cannot really see the issues and are in no positon to argue the point. Teenagers have enough cognitive development to see the sins of their parents and argue them, but society has ignored their complaints with the derogatory and dismissive cliché of "the teenage rebellion".

So it is up to parents to consider why a relationship that produces clichés such as the "terrible twos", the "sassy five year old" and the "teenage rebellion" has been perpetuated for so long and been so rarely challenged. This book will carry on this discussion and show that it is possible to raise a great child in a positive way without the traditional conflicts and dysfunctions between parents and children. You can make the "terrible twos" and the "teenage rebellion" clichés of the past by choosing a new starting point for your interactions with your child.

Don't settle for an okay relationship, choose and develop a great one.

Self-Fulfilling Prophecies

It seems illogical to accept a system that keeps generating the same conflicts generation after generation, but Parenting 101 is accepted because it forecasts the very problems it causes. The premature expectation that a two year old should be perfectly obedient and compliant feeds the self-fulfilling prophecy of the "terrible twos". A seemingly simple request unfulfilled, generates parental upset and a cycle of punishments and continuing unmet requests. It "proves" to the parent that all of the negative warnings about two year olds are true. This keeps reinforcing itself as more force and harshness is applied, and the child still does not comply (because of his immaturity, not stubbornness).

Instead of accepting the "terrible twos" prophecy, parents should question why their child would suddenly change from being sweet and innocent, to disobedient and quarrelsome. No one has suggested that there is a hormone surge to change their behavior. The tradition of the "terrible twos" suddenly appearing at two, overrides a more likely scenario of continued slow gaining of behavioral ability. Instead of perfect compliance at two, it should be expected that there will be fits and starts as the immature and imperfect child slowly matures.

By choosing a new starting point with the mindset that the child is innocent and doing the best that he can, the parent will more likely stay on a path of proactively solving the problem for and with the child. When parental requests are not met, solutions will be looked for that suit the child's abilities better instead of using penalties and threats and stubbornly trying to force compliance. Friendly help from the parent is better than angry insistence that the child should "get the job done or else".

You are not relaxing your rules, you are finding better ways to teach and reach them.

There are societies that make no demands on two year olds, and guess what? They do not have "the terrible twos". They have the same behavioral expectations for their two year olds as they do for their one and a half year olds, These parents remain responsible for maintaining their safety and the safety of others and things around them for another year. They do not have the conflicts that the premature demand and punishment method generates.

At three, the understanding parent looks back on

another happy year with their immature but improving child. The child has experienced another happy year with his parents. Now, they can cooperate more because they are more mature and developmentally able to understand, not because they have been "whipped into shape". More importantly, a friendly helpful pattern of parenting has been put in place.

As you read this book, critically examine the traditional assumptions about how to raise children Answering these questions with new eyes and being skeptical about traditional rules of parenting will help you to consider a new starting point with your child. Reject the self-fulfilling prophecies. Overcome the resistance to changing the status quo. Believe that you can raise a good and productive child with a friendly and proactive style that does away with contention and be her best friend and resource throughout her life.

A New Starting Point

- Present a friendly helpful face to your child when you are correcting him. Have a sense of humor. Remember he's the one you love more than anyone. The more you practice, the more natural it will become to have firm, but friendly interventions, rather than angry confrontations.
- Remember that your child's developmental stage limits his ability to respond appropriately to your demands. Consider that repeated failures to get cooperation most likely mean that the situation is over your child's head developmentally.
- The basic issues in big and little problems are similar and their correction is not too different, in principle.

We often inject more intensity in the bigger issues simply because of our sense of danger and insecurity.

- Help your child find a better course of action; do not just demand that he stop his bad conduct. Be a teacher/mentor and role model and show him the better way.

- Continue to stay within your standards for good behavior. Keep your standards for behavior high.

- Most importantly, remember that he is still developing his abilities. He may have done the right thing once, but it may take some time before you can assume that he will do it right consistently.

CHAPTER 7: KEY KNOWLEDGE - UNDERSTANDING BEHAVIORAL DEVELOPMENT

It is easier to build strong children than to repair broken men.

- Frederick Douglass

The lack of understanding of behavioral development is at the heart of most of the early conflicts in the parent-toddler relationship, and continues into teenage disputes.

We are looking at three areas of development in children, physical, cognitive, and behavioral. The developmental chart for reaching physical milestones is fairly concrete and not controversial. Most parents are clear when we should expect sitting, crawling, and walking and these landmarks can be easily found in standard pediatric books and a quick search of the internet.

Jean Piaget outlined the stages of cognitive development and the steps that lead to adult thinking and learning. Piaget's work also can be found summarized on the internet, and for the ambitious, you can read his book. One practicality of cognitive development can be measured against the child's progress in the educational system.

Deviations or delays in the areas of physical development and education accomplishment are readily apparent to the parents and generate a helpful and proactive response.

Parents are not as clear when behavioral milestones are attained; when their child has enough maturity to obey their orders, comply with their wishes, and be counted on to stay out of danger. In fact, these failures to comply are often seen as disobedience and defiance not developmental immaturity. Behavioral developments require time to reach maturation, just like physical and intellectual issues, and are actually more complex and difficult to perfect.

Rather than being treated as a developmental issue, our culture has made these impasses clichés of "inherent bad attitude stages". "As stated before, "the terrible twos" and "the teenage rebellion" have been etched in the stone of tradition. There is no sense that these stages could have been avoided by better parenting techniques. In fact, some parents are blamed for being too lax and soft (a self-fulfilling prophecy).

Variations in cultural and parental expectations make agreement on a universal timetable for behavioral milestones unlikely. Also, parents do not consistently agree on what they considered an acceptable response. An easy-going parent may accept a sloppy barely done job as a good try and an acceptable endpoint, while another more demanding parent will only accept a perfectly done job. The age of attainment of a given behavior is also not agreed upon, so, how can parents find and set a standard for their child and themselves?

First, make the assumption that your toddler is innocent. Realize that we are uncertain of his behavioral development abilities. Understand that he being physically capable of doing what you have demanded of him is really only the first step. He still must gain a sense of the importance and reasons for your commands and consistently carry them out.

Second, compare your trust in him handling a seemingly simple straightforward demand with an equally simple but potentially dangerous one. When we are feeling that our toddler is old enough to put her toys away, do we also feel that we can adequately instruct her to not to take medication that has been left out or cross a street safely?

Both are easily explained tasks, but there are many details that must be taken into account to do both things properly. Protecting the toddler from taking an overdose of medicine is so obviously the parent's responsibility, that the parent only blames themselves if an accident occurs. Putting toys away has no danger associated with it, but doing it neatly, promptly, and carefully every time requires an equal amount of behavioral maturity as avoiding carelessly left out medications. Thinking of dangerous situations provides a measure of how much you can depend on your child's maturity in carrying out everyday situations.

Third, observe a preschool of two, three, and four year olds playing together. You will see that each age (maturity) group handles the same task differently. After a short while you can accurately guess the age of a child by how he handles the task (regardless of the size of the child). It demonstrates that the ability to fulfill a request improves naturally with maturity. Compliance isn't fully developed at two or three when the parent starts demanding it. The two or three year old may understand that an unfriendly "no" is a signal of disapproval, but, she is far from knowing that it means not to do something now, later or forever.

Think of the gaining of a behavioral goal like a fund raising thermometer that depicts the rise in contributions collected. As the mark goes up, progress can be seen but it may be some time before we reach our 100% goal. So, it is with the child gaining the desired behavior, progress is being made with each incident, but it will take some time before we reach our goal. In the meantime, be patient and helpful, and smile.

CHAPTER 8: FACTORS CONFUSING THE UNDERSTANDING OF BEHAVIORAL STAGES

Behavioral developmental stages are not easily defined and many factors add to mudding the clarity of the situation even more.

These factors include:
- The danger level of a particular situation.
- The monetary value of the item
- The inconvenience of altering the situation.
- Social situations – the pressure we feel from others as we handle a problem with our child
- Stereotypical reactions to children versus adults
- Repeated misadventures, it's the situation, not the child
- Being proactive about developmental limitations

The Danger Level

The danger level is perhaps the easiest to illustrate. The dangers of poisoning, drowning, cutting oneself with a knife, and falling down stairs is so evident to the parent that he takes the responsibility of child-proofing without putting any responsibility on his child. The child is usually not even made aware of what the parent is doing in these situations.

But, in less dangerous situations, we make them responsible for outcome even though they are no more mature in their reasoning and awareness as in the more dangerous situation. In fact, the less dangerous situations are more subtle and harder to understand for the child. So, the toddler is scolded for picking leaves off grandma's plants or tearing a magazine or a book. On the other hand, we are upset with ourselves when we have forgotten to put a knife or medicine away. Why was it the child's fault in the first situation, but ours in the second one? The lack of danger does not make the child smarter.

A friend said that she acted very upset with her two-year-old son when he ran into the street while she was doing yard work. He continued to run away after she told him not to, and she got angrier and angrier with him. Shouldn't he have listened to her? But, how many times has he played this game of chase with his laughing parents, who caught him and tickled and hugged him again and again. Besides, has she and can she really adequately explain where the boundaries are in this situation?

Compare your yard and a swimming pool. With the simple change of the street to the swimming pool, the perceived danger of the situation is more obvious and threatening. Most people would not count on the child minding just because they were told to stay away from the pool. If they knew they would be distracted by yard work, they would hopefully make sure someone else was there to keep an eye on the child if there was nothing on or around the pool to keep the child from falling in.

Being hit by a car obviously can be just as tragic as a drowning, but for some reason many adults see these two dangers differently and put more of the blame on the child when he runs into the street. The child can put himself into a dangerous situation just as easily in either case. The question is not, shouldn't he listen to me? It's not about him; it's all about you. The question in the parent's mind should be, can I do a job in an unsecured setting and guarantee my toddler's safety at the same time? Just because you enjoy having him near you while you work in your own yard, does not mean that he will rise to the occasion and act better than his developmental age.

I was at a major league baseball game and saw a two-year-old dash away from her parents in the crowded refreshment area. The parents yelled loudly and harshly at her, and when they caught up with her they grabbed her hand forcefully and scolded her, telling her never to do that again. The safety of this two-year-old should not be in the child's own hands, but the parents.

This episode should be a wakeup call for the parents to be more protective in these situations. Speaking harshly and lecturing their two year old child to the dangers of running away is of no immediate value. The child is too immature not to be distracted again and to remember and follow the lessons. The conversation that should take place is between the parents of how they should watch and protect their immature child better.

The Monetary Cost of a Mistake

The expensive of an item presents a similar situation. We put an expensive vase out of the reach of the child without even thinking about it. The cost of the vase and the fact that the child has no need to deal with it makes it an easy choice to put it out of reach. It is so obvious that it is often done without a thought. On the other hand, if the item is not expensive, we may casually allow our child access to it, but still become upset if it is not handled appropriately.

Books are not so expensive and if torn can still be read or easily fixed. If they were bought for the child, we want him to have ready access to them. If the child continues to tear books even after we stop him, tell him that he needs to be more careful, and supervise him the next few times. Book publishers have realized what very young children might do to a book and have proactively made cloth books and sturdy cardboard books for them.

The Inconvenience of the Situation

In a surprisingly large number of cases, inconvenience is a big factor in how we react towards our children. When TVs and stereo systems were large and heavy they became areas where discipline often started because our toddlers couldn't resist touching them and we couldn't easily move or secure them. So it was common to hear raised voices and gentle or not so gentle tapping of their little hands. TVs are still big, but no longer have enticing knobs and buttons to push and pull. Remotes can be easily put out of reach. Audio equipment has become smaller and easier to move, so conflict has lessened there as well. These areas are no longer issues because of better technology, not better parenting.

A mother was asking how to discipline her two-year-old for climbing up a ladder in the garage. She and I had talked about not punishing, and being proactive instead. It was the first time that she had given her daughter a timeout. "You know, it was something really dangerous and I felt that I needed to emphasize how dangerous it was." "Did she learn her lesson," I asked. "Actually, I don't think she knew what it was all about, but I felt that it was important enough to do something. What else could I have done? I've been feeling subtle pressures from the grandmas to apply more discipline."

This mother disciplined her daughter with her first timeout because she wanted to be sure that she wouldn't do it again and hurt herself. When I pointed out that it may be hard to move the ladder but that it was unlikely to be impossible to do, it was like a bulb lighting. "Now I feel bad that I punished her for my laziness," but, she added, "I'll know better next time." I think that an added factor in this was that she had earlier mentioned that both grandmas felt that she didn't discipline enough.

It's always amazing to me how often an unusual situation can be brought up in a cluster. Two different mothers related that they had to discipline their child who was in the back seat of their car and opened their door while the car was in motion. They both told me that it was the exception to not punishing or yelling at them. They were relieved (and embarrassed) when we showed them the built-in locking mechanism in the backseat doors. Still, it was a little disturbing that they were counting on fear of punishment to keep their child from falling out of the car.

Social Situations and Relationships

Social situations and relationships can also impact what parents expect from their children and how they discipline them. One common influence is relatives, especially your own parents if they still believe in stronger and earlier disciplining than you do. Remember, they were probably stronger believers in the terrible twos. (I must interject in defense of my fellow grandparents that we have generally mellowed considerably, and often are pleading the case for leniency.) But, when the criticism comes from the grandparents it is hard to ignore (or take).

The disapproval of our peers is also hard to deal with at times. It is difficult to stick to your standards when another parent is glaring at you over an incident involving her child and yours. Instead of simply fixing the problem some parents will scold their child first, when they normally would not have without this peer pressure.

The type of social situation can also influence how parents deal with their children. At our grandson's second birthday party a young woman came to lead the kids in games and songs. She wanted them to get into a line like a train and go around the yard. There were younger and older siblings there in addition to the two-year-old guests.

A one year old was carried up in his father's arms, and the rest were told to get in line. It was soon clear that the parents of the two-year-olds needed to help get them organized. The three-year-olds got in line by themselves, but started to wander as things were being slowly put together. The only child that knew what to do was a four-year-old, who tried to help get the younger kids to stay in place. It was a beautiful demonstration of how your developmental age determines your capabilities and limitations.

The other remarkable point was that the parents were all helping with a smile on their faces, without a hint of a threat or sternness, even when their child was slow to respond. After all, they were trying to help them have fun.

Is it unfair to imagine that the parents might have been sterner and upset and threatening if instead of helping the kids to have fun, they were faced with the social issue of trying to get their reluctant children to help clean up at the end of the party? Here the social pressure can make them look at their children's reactions differently.

Reactions to Children Versus Adults

Children's actions are often unconsciously judged differently within the same context that an adult would be judged, especially when virtues, compliance, and respect are involved. These issues are so important to the parent that when they come up, the parent tries to teach a lesson to their child without fully considering the immaturity of the child.

Paradoxically, many times we are more understanding with adults than children. If our child knocks over a glass of water at a restaurant, we are apt to scold him for being careless and give him a look of disappointment and exasperation. But if an adult makes the same mistake, we would usually laugh and joke about it.

The restaurants are clear on the issue and often ahead of our request will automatically give the child a plastic cup with a lid (that's difficult to dislodge) and a straw. It is instructive that the restaurant industry and book publishers understand the limitations of our young children and proactively take steps that recognize their developmental limitations. I doubt that they are smarter than the average parent, but they have learned from seeing many young kids spill their drinks and have taken a proactive approach of making it less likely that they will have a mess to clean up.

When we hire an adult to work in our office, we want him to work within our guidelines just as we expect of our children. The difference is that when the adult does not do his work properly, we stop him and then explain what we want. There is no threat of punishment, only explanation and encouragement. With our child, who is much less capable, we expect more. Part of the reason for this is our greater personal investment in our child than a stranger we have hired, but still it is puzzling that we tend to be harder on the one we care about more.

An adult going to his first formal dinner can rise to the occasion and learn how to comport himself. But, a three-year-old might not get through a long dinner at a nice restaurant no matter how much we berate him and insist that he rise to the occasion (our needs). The wise parent after one such misadventure will either get a babysitter or have a plan for taking the child out of the situation from time to time. They understand that developmentally he is not ready to get through the long dinner and act proactively to make the situation easier for both them and their child..

This is a good example of how parents can intuitively understand the issue of developmental stage and ability to perform. Unfortunately, there are many other situations where we are in conflict with our child because we are not clear on those circumstances and still expect then to rise to the occasion.

Repeated Misadventures, It's the Situation, Not the Child

If a parent is consistently encountering problems in relation to a particular situation, there is a good chance that the problem is the situation, not the child. A mother related to me that she had been having conflicts with her three-and-a-half year old daughter every morning while getting her ready for school. It all got better when she took a few minutes to think about the root of the problem. The mom realized that she was depending heavily on her daughter to take care of herself in the morning because she had to help her disabled older son and her baby get dressed.   The fact that her daughter is so precocious in many ways led her to be unrealistic about how capable her daughter was of getting herself ready in the morning. So, after a quick brainstorming session, the mom decided to start the process in the morning 15 minutes earlier and help her daughter first. Now her daughter was not only ready for the day, she could help her mother with her less capable siblings. Everyone was happier. She solved the problem, rather than creating more conflict by insisting and threatening.

A father once said to me that he understood that his two-year-old was innocent, but that the child had started "testing limits" by throwing his food on the floor and laughing. He related this in a good-humored way. Dad was on the right track with his attitude, but he was still attributing a negative behavior to his son that he really did not have. The child was not doing anything as complex as testing limits or pushing buttons. He does not even have a clue what these terms mean.

What actually was happening was something far more

straightforward. The child had finished eating and he wanted the plate out of his way. No more, no less. It is a purely immature, but practical decision to remove what he no longer needs. He is disposing of it in a way that makes more work for his father, but it does not mean that he is pushing buttons or tweaking his patient father on purpose. He is doing what a lot of two-year-olds would do. He is acting his developmental age. You can be proactive and remove the plate before it becomes an issue. But have you missed an opportunity to teach a life lesson? Many feel that they could have highlighted this situation with anger and threats, but at his age, the only thing he would learn is to be fearful of his parent's wrath.

When the children are not handling a situation, assume, or at least, consider that for whatever reason they are not up to the task, rather than just being non-compliant and help them or alter the situation.

Being Proactive About Developmental Limitations

Thinking ahead about what may happen and planning how to change or handle a possible problem helps to avoid problems. Start by considering if your child's behavioral developmental stage can handle the task. If you are not sure, take the responsibility to make the situation more child-friendly. Sometimes the best solution is to wait a few more months until your child's development stage matches the situation that we are asking him to handle

If you are dreading going to a social occasion with your toddler, doesn't it make sense to have a plan that suits your child's abilities rather than just hope for the best.

In many cases the parent has the option to put her child in a situation that allows the child to act her age with or without conflict. Imagine you have two-year-old twins and you and your spouse have two choices for what to do with them. One of you takes one child to the park and the other takes one child shopping for wedding presents. Which parent would most likely have more fun with their child? This is not a trick question, by the way.

The child and parent who went to the park had a wonderful day running, laughing, and screaming with joy. The parent who had the more difficult day in a crowded store and ended up punishing the child for too much touching and disobedience might take some satisfaction that she reprimanded her child and taught a lesson about how to behave. Does this mean that the child who had a fun day missed out on a learning opportunity and now is not as informed or mature as her twin? Nope, they are still the same age and maturity, give or take a few minutes. These misadventures have not made the child who experienced them any more mature or capable. They are still limited by their developmental stage.

If every trip to the grocery store with your two-year-old is an unpleasant event that should tell you that the situation does not work for either her or you. Having so many tempting things to grab and not being able to run around can make it a constant struggle, especially in a crowded store. The usual response is, "I have to shop and can't hire a babysitter just to do that." Does this mean that your needs must be satisfied even if there's been a pattern of your child being yelled at and punished?

This is a situation that gets better results by thinking out the situation ahead of time and being proactive. There are other choices for grocery shopping, such as having both parents go to the store; one parent shops while the other watches the child. Or, shop at a time when the other parent can be at home with the child. Or, go at an off time when the store is not as busy and you do not feel pushed. Usually these mundane trips are not planned. Often they are done spontaneously from the parent's point of view, without considering that another plan or time might work better for all parties involved. Developing a proactive plan to make it work better for your child usually becomes a win-win situation. Just by waiting, it won't be long before your child has matured and your shopping trips will be fun for you and your little helper.

The Parent's State of Mind

The parent's state of mind is an important, but often neglected factor. Impulsive, negative exchanges with your child are not the best thing for them, but give yourself a break, you give up so much of yourself every day to your child that you can be forgiven your cranky, short-tempered moments.

Some parents have become so hypercritical of themselves that they are putting disapproving mothers-in-laws out of work. More seriously, many have been distraught that these moments have ruined their day. Yes, you were less than perfect and you'll get a grade of 92 for the day. Our children will thrive with parents who get A minuses for their day's work–even B pluses.

It is important for you to pay attention to your needs, and seek advice when the going seems to be getting you down too much and too often. Parents have a duty to give up a lot of their time to their children, but should save time for themselves. The best thing that you can give your child is a happy parent.

Summary

- A child's developmental abilities must mature before he can learn and perform.
- If you are unsure of your child's developmental abilities, start by thinking of your child as innocent and doing the best that she can; that your child is neither morally bad nor good.
- The more mature person, you, has the ability to make it work. You can manage the situation and instruct your child and advance them.
- Be aware of those factors that can cloud your judgment.
- Be proactive. Look for solutions to potentially difficult situations ahead of time and adjust for them.
- Sometimes you just need to get through the moment as best as you can; a few more months of maturity (theirs, not yours) will make things work better.
- Children do not learn a lesson from just one experience. The next time they may not do it right. Keep realistic expectations based on their developmental stage. Give them time to grow into your expectations.
- Take care of yourself.

CHAPTER 9: THE PROACTIVE PARENT

Anyone who does anything to help a child is a hero to me.
-   Fred Rogers

Early in my career, a mother came to my pediatric office to talk about how poorly her son was doing as a high school sophomore. She said that his performance this year was so miserable that she could hardly speak to him without anger, and he was returning the favor. They had hardly exchanged a civil word for the last month.

"Didn't you use to get along well with him?" I asked.

"Yes," she replied, "and that's making it even worse, remembering how much fun we used to have. Now he gets home, and I ask him how much homework he has, and he doesn't answer and heads to his bedroom. I try to check to make sure he's doing his work, but he just gets angrier with me. Obviously, he's not doing the work, because his last report card had a C and the rest D's. I'm not sure what else I can do to get him to do his work. I've already taken away most of his privileges, but that hasn't had any effect, except more anger. I keep warning him that he's not going to get into a good college like his sisters did, but he says he doesn't care."

This mom was about my age, and I had always admired her lively and well behaved children. I told her that, to be honest, I was not sure what to suggest. So we did a little brainstorming and tried to figure out what was wrong. As we talked, it became clear that her goals were good, but she was sacrificing the positive aspects of their relationship for the sake of making her son a better student at any cost. "Education is so important," she said. "I hate to see him waste his chances of getting into a good school."

This mother's tactics might have made some sense if, in fact, their conflict had resulted in her son improving his grades, but the opposite was true. Besides, I asked her, "even if he did make good grades, was it worth it to have him angry at her all the time?" Moreover, was it reasonable to expect this kind of constant conflict would result in better grades?

The mother's emphasis on grades and college had made her relationship with her son secondary to his academic achievements. After some discussion we came to the conclusion that the most important issue was to fix their broken relationship. She had to get in touch again with what she had known and felt before, that nothing is more valuable to a child than a good relationship with his parent. To regain his trust, she had to turn their relationship around.

I gave this mother some suggestions about how she could go about repairing the damage and reestablishing their relationship. "First," tell your son how much you love him and want him to succeed. Let him know that all the bickering over school was causing you to be angry with each other, and that you want that to stop. Tell him you've decided you're not going to discuss anything about school with him until you both enjoy the conversation and get back to where you were before."

"But what if he continues to do poorly in school?" she asked.

I replied that, by all indications, her current plan was a flop. There wasn't anything to lose by trying something new. I suggested that there was a safety net. Even with poor grades, he could get into a junior college, where he would have a second chance to do well. She decided to try this new approach. Even if her son's grades didn't improve, at least they might be talking to each other again.

This interaction was my introduction to proactive parenting. This wise mother was able to stop and seek help so she could assess her difficulties with her son. Our conversation led her to realize that she was the one who had to make the changes to repair their relationship. It was up to her. It wasn't about who was right or wrong. She realized it was about who could initiate change. She could righteously demand that her son shape up all she wanted to, but realistically, she was the only one mature enough to change the dynamics of their relationship. Once she recognized this, she became proactive and made the appropriate changes.

She didn't have to change the family's standards for behavior. Instead, she changed her parenting style from demanding to helpful. Rather than demand that her son perform, she enabled him to perform. She made their relationship a primary concern. She expressed a genuine interest in his point of view. Then she adopted a mentoring and teaching approach to help him. .Her actions convinced him that she was there to help him.

Typically, it does not take long to see the benefits of

being proactive. In this example, the mother reported that her loving relationship with her son returned relatively quickly with her change in attitude. Changing her attitude from demanding to helping was probably the hardest thing to do. Breaking old patterns and habits of Parenting 101 is not easy, but once you feel comfortable in your new starting point, it can become your natural path.

Everyday life became less confrontational for them and a spirit of cooperation started to return. His school work returned to its former high level and culminated in him reaching his college goals. The mother was once again an important influence in her son's life because she was helpful, not demanding. He again allowed himself to be guided by her wisdom and experience. She saw that parenting was about helping your child to succeed, not just pleasing your parent.

The benefits of proactive parenting can be far reaching. In this case, although the basic change was in the mother-son relationship, that change created a new starting point for better family relationships and more productive interactions in school and at home. Moreover, the changes this mother initiated in her family will likely be carried on by all of her children when they become parents, and thus continue to benefit future generations.

The Principles of Proactive Parenting

As I have encouraged parents to take a more proactive approach to issues with their children, some basic principles have become apparent.

A Proactive Parent Takes Responsibility for Making the Relationship with Her Child Work

A proactive parent has the power and the duty to change a situation that is not working for the parent and/or the child. This means that, as a proactive parent, you should take the responsibility for initiating the adjustments that make the situation better, not just demand that your child listen to you. It is too easy to take the traditional parental position that you are right and he is wrong and that he needs to change. It is up to you to keep an eye out for possible problems and solutions. In this way, some problems can be identified and solved before they become confrontations. Almost always, if you take a proactive stance and continue to problem solve, you can find an alternative solution that will be acceptable to both you and your child.

A Proactive Parent Earns the Admiration, Respect, and Trust of the Child. One Wonderful Day Your Child Will Return It

Respect for each other starts with the parent respecting the child. Parents are not due the respect of their child just because they are the parents. Among our peers, we respect a friend because of the good deeds we see him do for us and others, not because he has more power than we do and can bully us. Similarly, your child will admire, respect, and trust you if she sees that you are there to be helpful, rather than just critical of her missteps. Your child will grow up feeling that you are willing to listen to her, and knowing that it will always be possible to get useful advice from you.

As she matures and understands how you respect her, she will reciprocate. Best of all you will have preserved her confidence in herself.

A Proactive Parent Needs to Show, Model, and Teach the Better Way

You can't expect your young child to get something right just because you insisted she must act a certain way. First you must be clear that her developmental abilities are up to the task you are asking her to do. Stopping bad behavior is essential, but it is just the starting point of educating your child to do the right thing.

As a proactive parent, you take on the roles of model, teacher, and mentor. When your child sees you in this light, she will be more comfortable and responsive than if you assume the role of strict disciplinarian. You want your child to do the right thing because she understands that what you are teaching is a better way to approach a problem, not because she fears a possible punishment.

Fear of discipline often leads to deception and hiding of mistakes.

A Proactive Parent Is in Charge, but Stops and Listens to Their Child

Certainly, adults should be in charge of their children, but this does not mean you can or should automatically reject or ignore your child's suggestions or complaints. Stop to consider whether there is any validity to a protest, or if you are asking too much of your child. Stop and listen to her view point, it doesn't cost you anything.

Don't act insulted that you are being questioned. Some

parents, even when they realize they are wrong, still insist that their child needs to listen to them and respect their authority. They are acting under the old rules that made parental authority something to always defend. Parents have so much power that being able to admit their mistakes usually strengthens their stature in the eyes of their children, rather than weakens it.

A Proactive Parent Gets Her Just Rewards

I had a round table discussion with medical students about this book and the theme of moving away from crime and punishment. One of the students related, "I was pretty rebellious and it was probably good that my parents punished me to keep me in line. His experiences growing up were probably in the "annoyed with his parents but still aware that his parents loved him" category. The negative consequence for him was that he probably had five or six years of conflict and loss of good advice from his parents in those crucial teenage years. Further, he will probably continue his parent's pattern of parenting because his perception of his upbringing is that their harsh treatment kept him in line and helped him to turn out okay.

In counterpoint another student related how she was very late coming home one night and quietly crept into her house only to be met with the sight of her mother sleeping on the sofa in the living room. When her mother awoke, much to this student's surprise, instead of expressing upset with her, her mother expressed great relief that she was home safely. The student stated that her mother's understanding of and concern for her, rather than anger over breaking her rules, led her to never want to disappoint her mother again. She said she got through the tough times in her life because she knew that if she needed them, her parents would always be there for her, helpful and positive, not judgmental or threatening and disapproving of her failures. Both of these individuals have succeeded in a highly competitive field, but, I believe the road was harder for the young man because of his parent's harsher methods. Will he be there for his children when they need him?

The Wild Card – Love

I think the young man was still able to lead a productive life because of what we might call the wild card in the parent-child relationship. That wild card is the overwhelming love parents have for their child. It is the elephant in the room in a good way. The parent's love for her child is always present even though it may not be obvious to the young child during a dispute If their contention and tensions have not been too severe, the child grows up accepting the bad with the good because of the ever present love, and doesn't allow the conflicts to completely ruin their relationship. . It makes up for a lot of imperfect parenting.

The parent's proactive manner of communication and relationship is all important. It should consistently be friendly and helpful, not demanding and threatening. The child will learn to never doubt their parent's love for her. She will begin to understand that "whenever I have a problem, my parents will always be there to help me."

Summary

The Proactive Parent

- Proactive parents take responsibility for making the relationship with their child mutually happy and satisfying
- The proactive parent understands child development
- Let's nothing stand in the way of her child understanding that you love her
- Respect for each other starts with the parent respecting the child.
- Modeling and mentoring, and teaching are the tools of proactive parenting
- A friendly and caring relationship should be obvious to the child.
- Do not settle for an "okay" relationship, strive for a great one

CHAPTER 10: MENTORING AND TEACHING

Don't walk behind me: I may not lead. Don't walk
in front of me, I may not follow. Just walk beside
me and be my friend.

- Albert Camus

Your Best Teacher

Think back to your best teacher. She was tough and
something of a perfectionist, and settled for nothing but
your best. There was no compromising on her principles.
You still enjoyed the class and admired the teacher because
you learned so much. Her secret? While she was exacting
and stopped you whenever you made a mistake, she never
belittled or threatened you. Instead, you knew that as
uncompromising as she was, she cared about you and
would give you the help that you needed. Not too little, not
too much, but just right. She knew how to position you to
do the job, not take over the job.

This is the opposite of the approach that seems to have
dominated the traditional practices of Parenting101. There

was a sense that you could not let your child get away with making mistakes, that there needed to be a show of disapproval and a consequence to make sure that they would remember not to do it again.

Teaching your child how to do something the right way requires making one or two points. While the child may repeat her errors because of her immaturity, you just need to stick to your rules and repeat what you have said until your lessons are clearly understood.

The Path of Teaching and Mentoring

How often have you seen a toddler grab what his baby sister has and trade it for whatever he does not want at the moment, rather than just taking the toy he wants? This is a product of your modelling and teaching. He learned that from you. Not perfect, but getting there. You should help your child learn how to deal with the problem facing him and teach him how to handle it in the context of your broader view of what is fair and important in life.

Children, at first, do not really realize that you smoothed over their squabbles with their friends and siblings. They do not notice that you set your limits without being angry and punitive.

Later they do become aware that there are limits in their lives that you enforce, but that you also give explanations and other choices. They see that they can question your rules and get a reasonable and friendly answer. They find that they can, at times, persuade you to their way of thinking. They become more comfortable talking to you about their concerns and issues. They feel good, or at least okay, after talking with you, and never feel demeaned. They see you as a resource of good and helpful advice. Your thoughtful behavior is returned to you.

Teaching and mentoring are methods that carry goodwill along with the lessons that they impart. They help to advance our children's behavior and life skills in a proactive and positive way. These methods open up the world for your child, while the crime and punishment approach only narrows their world. Best of all, your love for our child is not obscured by anger and disapproval. Your children understand that you want to help them and love them.

The voices of the past say that a parent cannot be effective and be their child's friend. They say there must be some emotional distance between them. But, who do you love more in your world than your family? The challenge is to learn how to be a friend and an effective parent at the same time. You can adopt the model of your best teacher and you can become your child's best teacher in life.

Making Sure Your Message Is Clear

When I was teaching residents at Oakland Children's Hospital, one of the residents laughed about an encounter with a grandmother and her grandson who had an ear infection. She had come back several days later upset that the medicine her grandson had been given did not seem to be working. Well, he laughed, would you believe she was putting the oral medicine into his ear canal? His senior resident was not laughing, and interjected, "you really did a poor job for this patient." The intern was taken aback, and protested by saying he had told them exactly what to do. The senior resident responded by saying, "I'm sure that you did, but your job was not just to tell her what to do, it was to be sure that she clearly understood what you told her and that the child got the medicine correctly. This you didn't do."

So it is with parents. It is your job not only to say the right words, but to make sure that your words are fully understood. Considering if your child's has the capacity to truly understand your words and intent helps to make your requests realistic and achievable.

A ten-year-old boy was dared by his friends to say something sexually inappropriate to a girl in his class. The girl promptly reported it to their teacher and the boy's parents had to meet with the principal. On the way home, the parents asked if he knew what the words he said meant. He said no. His father said, "I think a good punishment would be no cell phone for two week, so he can think about what he did." His mother interceded and suggested, "instead of just punishing him I think it would be better to talk to him about the situation and let him know that what he did was wrong, and teach him how to stand up to peer pressure."

This story summarizes the mentoring and teaching technique:
- Support your child
- Discuss the situation
- Keep your limits
- Teach a better way
- Let him know you love him

Mentoring at School

There are subtle situations that happen at school that inadvertently become crime and punishment scenarios at their heart. A parent asked me for advice about her first-grade son. He was not getting his work done, and his teacher had called her in to discuss what to do.

His teacher said that he really was not a disciplinary problem and that she really liked him. He just seemed to do anything but finish his work. As an "incentive", the teacher would allow him to go out for recess only if he had finished his work. She had chosen this because she knew how much he loved to play and run outside and didn't really want to punish him. But that did not seem to work, so she had called in his parents. The mother pointed out, "lately, he did not seem to like going to school."

Is it any wonder that he was not having a happy school experience? The teacher felt she was offering an incentive, going out to play, instead of punishing him for his lack of work, but everyone else was going out to play. The teacher meant well, but was concentrating so much on what she thought was a good and easy solution that she did not address the real issue of how to help him. And she did not see that she was, in fact, punishing the child. Withholding a privilege is a backhanded punishment, but it is a punishment nonetheless.

Take another case of a seven-year-old boy's slowness in getting his daily class work done. He was known to be a very bright boy and quite capable of doing the work. Again, recess was taken away, and because that did not help, the school called a meeting with the parents. The teacher and principal sat in, and the principal kindly asked the boy if he could think of ways to improve. The boy had a deer-in-the-head-lights look, under the pressure, could not respond, and was on the verge of tears.

What is common to these approaches is that the school is neither teaching nor mentoring. Many times they do not recognize that they are using coercion, not teaching. They are trying to get the child to respond to what they would call an incentive, which for all practical purposes is a punishment.

The authority figures involved might argue that they are not punishing, only trying to give positive incentives. This was a common theme in books some years ago, to praise the positive and eliminate the negative. But, in these cases the positive incentives clearly have a negative side. Even if you don't have an actual negative consequence in mind, isn't the withholding of the positive still the same as a negative? To these children, withholding a positive incentive, being able to play with their friends, certainly doesn't feel positive or even neutral.

A proactive approach would be to make the child aware of the importance of getting his work done in the allotted time and coach him a few times. He may not be totally clear that getting the work done in a timely way is an important part of the lesson. Another child of about the same age was told that she needed to get her work done faster. Her response was to do it much faster, but with many more mistakes and illegible handwriting. Back to the drawing board.

In these cases, the teachers are not addressing the fact that these children are not mature enough yet to fully understanding what is wanted of them. Making the child guess what the principal is thinking is not helpful. Instead of interrogating them and trying to get them to guess what you are thinking, why not use simple statements that explain the problem and give them some helpful suggestions. This is more direct and has the element of being helpful without the pupil feeling he must come up with the right answer. This is mentoring and teaching.

Your Child Comes First in School Conflicts

Often a note from the teacher explains a disciplinary issue that she wants you to help reinforce at home. You like the teacher, know that your wonderful child can be wild and crazy at times, so you do not hesitate to try to help the teacher. But, before you start to deal with the problem, think about how this all lines up.

If you start from the teacher's point of view, and tell your child how upset you are about his behavior, and that you are going to punish him in some way to reinforce the school's position, who does he have on his side? He has already been reprimanded and feels threatened by the second biggest authority figure in his world, and now the biggest (you) is going to do the same.

Do you let him get away with it or join forces with the teacher? No and no, there is a third choice. You can first tell him, "I understand how badly you must have felt to have your nice teacher be upset with you. Here, sit down and I'll help you figure out how to have a better day tomorrow."

Your child understands that you are considering his side and helping him first and you are still helping the teacher solve her problem   How great to know that your parents are always there to help you.

The mother of a good spirited, outgoing boy who was full of life, as I saw him, was told that the school had an issue with him. Their family appreciated their school and the teacher, and so was distressed that they were upset with him. She told me, "that it just did not seem like him." I said, "If it doesn't seem like him, what makes you think that the school is right?" With that she brightened up and thought about the issues in a whole different light, from her son's perspective. She went to the school clearly on behalf of her son and resolved the issue in a way that served her son first, and the school as well.

Summary

- Teaching and mentoring are far more informative and effective than threatening and punishing.
- You can explain the right way once or try to stop the wrong way many times and ways
- Teaching and mentoring infuse your relationship with good will and cooperation.
- When dealing with problems at school, be sure that your child understands you are on his side and are there to help him solve his problem
- "Smile when you say that"

CHAPTER 11: "BUT"

I have had these discussions with many patients and friends and have had fairly universal agreement that this proactive, kinder approach was a better way. To my dismay, more than a few have added, "BUT, there are those times that a strong punishment is needed." Didn't we just spend 15 minutes talking about not punishing? "Yeah, but you know there are those times." I have discussed these issues in many different ways still there are the "BUTS".

This is a good time to pause and reassess and summarize what we have presented in the previous chapters.

Reluctance to wholeheartedly embrace a non-punitive approach comes from traditional positions that are so ingrained that it is hard to change attitudes with a conversation or two. Traditional parenting is a self-fulfilling prophecy of conflict that is very difficult to change. The traditional stance of absolute parental authority is subconsciously supported and reinforced by everyday jargon and clichés that have not been openly examined and vetted out of everyday conversations. Some parents don't even state their problems, they just say with a knowing tone in their voices, "Yeah, I have a two or three year old", as if it explains everything and condolences are automatically in order. The same goes for teenagers, but with more eyeball rolling. At adult gatherings it was (is) common to hear statements tossed out casually denigrating their toddlers and teenagers. Parents with children who I knew were great, when challenged, would back-peddle and admit, "they actually are pretty good". So why casually say something negative about them at all?

It comes from clichés like the terrible twos and the rebellious teenager. These time-honored clichés gave cover to the parent, implying that problems with children just were a passing natural phase of life, and not their fault or even the child's. While it isn't really helpful to blame either side, it perpetuates the problems because "it is natural and can't be helped and families just need to get through these rough times as best they can." Traditional parenting practices do not imply that parents need to find solutions by changing their methods and approach. The traditional advice is to stay the course, no matter how rocky. Don't give in.

There is also the sense that we naturally know how to parent because we have experienced it and even if we had problems with our parents, as we grew older we saw the need if not the wisdom of their methods. Our standards and moral guidelines are set in our minds and we just need to ensure that our children understand them. Traditionally, this is done by parents demanding behaviors and enforcing them with punishments when the demands are not met.

Timing Is Everything

Most parents have a good moral compass and want

nothing more than for their child to grow to be a successful, happy person. Traditional parenting has been about achieving or instilling these ends by enforcing compliance and obedience. This has been the state of affairs that justified the harsh penalties that good parents used to get their goals. Unfortunately it seemed that the goals of obedience and compliance were more important than the lessons being taught. That is, respect of the parent and his position of authority became the primary concern. Society at the same time sensed that harsh, especially physical punishment was unreasonable. But, what was reasonable? If the children didn't obey verbal orders didn't a parent have to, albeit reluctantly, finally resort to a punishment to get results? Society has gone down this path of looking for kinder ways to deal with these impasses with their children. But, these are not the issues at the heart of the problem.

Timing is the key issue that has been neglected. Parental goals for their children are usually good. The problem is that the parent tries to put them in place before the child is developmentally mature enough to understand the reasons placed upon them. The parent tries to enforce a rule that they feel is a very important lifelong principle and they lose sight of the fact that their child is not mature enough to understand the issues or need to comply. When the young child does not comply with the demands of the parent, visions of the teenage rebellion spring into the parent's mind and swift penalties are threatened and imposed. And so we have an exasperated and angry parent and a sullen defeated child who feels unloved as a result of bad timing.

That is why it is so important to really understand the behavioral development of our children. Children may do things right, even perfectly at times, but they need more time and experience to be consistent. A three year old waiting at a street corner and crossing when the light turns green on one occasion, hopefully, doesn't give a parent confidence that the child can be left to do it correctly the next time. The harshness of traditional parenting stems from this premature belief that the child should know better and anger and punishments are justified.

When the child does not comply to simple orders, it is better to assess whether or not we are asking too much of the child. Can you assume that he will cross the street safely or does he need to demonstrate further to you that he is completely mature and dependable in this act? While we may be annoyed with our child if he doesn't put his toys away after playing, we are more apt to blame ourselves for a mishap crossing a street. The danger factor clarifies our view of our child's developmental abilities, or lack thereof. The lack of danger and the everyday issue of putting toys away causes a parent to forget that developmental immaturity is the problem, not a stubborn child. Even a little demanded too soon can start a pattern of increasing harshness, punishments, and resentment. A strong willed child may dig in their heels because of the harsh treatment.

When an impasse comes about, stop and think if this simple request is still not within the developmental abilities of your child. Maybe your aiding with the task with good humor will help by modeling the correct behavior, rather than standing there and demanding in a stern unfriendly way.

The problem is that the emphasis is placed on obedience and compliance by the parent without a clear understanding of all of the factors involved. The importance of maintaining discipline is such a strong tenet of traditional parenting that little attention is given to more subtle, but more important issues. The timing of teaching coping methods and dealing with the feelings of the child are not emphasized enough.

When parents are struggling with disobedience and noncompliance, the general sense of tradition is to be tougher and stricter. Grandparents and peers who have older children often are giving this advice not to be soft on your rules for your children, but, timing and methods are more important than compliance and obedience in dealing effectively with teaching your children the rules of civility and good conduct and at the same time maintaining their self-esteem. The goal should not be gaining a compliant and obedient child, it should be to teach and mentor them to handle issues in their lives in a responsible and appropriate way because they see the value in what they are doing.

The importance of the issue sometimes blinds the parent to the limiting abilities of the immature child to act appropriately. And at times the failure to do the right thing is overshadowed by what the parent sees as acts of noncompliance and disobedience by the child.

As discussed in other chapters, mentoring, modelling and teaching done in a friendly atmosphere is the best and most effective approach. When this is not working, it is usually because the timing is bad, that is, we are trying to impart lessons before the child is developmentally ready to absorb them and follow and implement them. Some parents are very frustrated when the lesson is not learned because they were more patient and understanding than usual and the child did not change. "I was extra understanding and patient and it got me nowhere!!" Traditional parenting is vindicated, but actually the child was too immature to take on the lesson, even though the parent was kinder and more thoughtful than usual.

Kudos for trying a kinder, gentler approach, but again the problem is not the method, it is the timing. The patiently given lesson was still given too early for the child's developmental age. Being nicer and more patient is great, but still won't help make the point if the child is too immature to really understand your points. Also as noted out before, doing something right once doesn't mean that the immature child can be counted on to always do it right in the future. Compliance is not a direct and automatic result of increased kindness.

Change is hard when tradition has given you all the power and it seems you must give up this position and share the power with your child. This is not the case, it is asking parents to look at parenting in a different way. It is not about power. You are still in charge and still set the pattern of your family, but instead of simply demanding compliance and obedience from your child and threatening consequences and punishments if your wishes are not met, you first learn your child's developmental stage and capabilities. Then you time your teaching and mentoring accordingly and keep in mind maintaining their self-esteem while imparting your lessons in life.

The goal is to help your child to become a good and productive and resilient person Forcing your child to obey and comply by use of demands under threat of punishment only temporarily gets the behavior you want. Depending on how harsh the encounter was, there may also be anger and alienation and loss of self-esteem.

Parents should make their goal to teach and mentor their children to handle difficult situations properly, not just getting compliance and obedience. The parent's ego is served by acts of compliance and obedience. Solving the problems by parental knowledge of behavioral development and leadership through mentoring and teaching serves and grows the child, and the parent-child relationship.

"SHEEP DIP"

Parents are conditioned by tradition to resist change or even listening to a thoughtful discussion of changing their parenting methods because of the strong grip that Parenting 101 has in our culture. When I was a kid we would tease our friends by threatening to throw them into sheep dip. Being city boys, we really didn't know what it meant, but we imagined that you were going to be completely immersed into something stinky, disgusting, and hard to get off of you.

Parenting 101 may not exactly be sheep dip, but, parents have grown up in it and have become thoroughly covered in all of its sticky rules and regulations, and assumptions, and clichés, and jargon that justify it. Parenting 101 has been practiced by our great grandparents, grandparents and parents and its traditions are hard to escape.

At the same time we all seem to know a few families that look and act like a happy sit-com family. They are often dismissed as being lucky to have nice easy kids. Less credit is given to the kids having great parents. Advice is not often asked of them and when it is, it is quickly put aside when the parents suggest a more child-friendly approach to conflict. The question the embattled parent most often wants answered is "how do I make my child listen? It is not, "What am I doing wrong?"

The methods of these outliers, the happier families, need to be examined by the less happy families. These outliers have rejected the idea that conflict is unavoidable, and have sought and found friendlier ways to raise good and productive children.

Finding how to establish this "sweet spot" for your

family from day one is crucial because acceptance of conflict as "natural and unavoidable" allows family conflicts to grow and become harder and harder to reverse. We need to rid ourselves of traditional "sheep dip."

CHAPTER 12: SIBLING RELATIONSHIPS

You know how that feels?

- Gary D. Schmidt
  Okay For Now

The First Child

Learning how to become a great parent is the theme of this book. We have gone over parenting in an overall way. However, there are some specific points that apply more directly to the first child, the greatest challenge for the parent. The enormity of this job at some point hits the new parents like a ton of bricks. The parent has usually had little training to do this task and survives mostly with vague past memories and on-the-job training.

Generally, the first child will be the most protected and hovered over. This happens because the parent is anxious about her abilities as a new parent and has time to micro-manage every move that the child makes. Often the first child is not allowed as much spontaneous activity as his future siblings will have. As a two or three year old, he will tend to wait for his parents to initiate activities and encourage or even force him to try something new. He will often hang back when he is presented with new activities. I encourage parents to put their first children into group activities without asking their child, if they think he would enjoy it, because his answer will often be an automatic no.

Is this fair to do? I would say it is. We send our children to pre-school or a babysitter without asking for their agreement because we have to, or feel it is important. Even though recreational activities are optional, the child at this age does not really understand what he is agreeing or refusing to do. It is mostly an automatic shying away from anything new and unknown and away from his parents.

The parent is really in the best position to decide how well the activity will work. She knows that several of his friends will be there, and that the coach is a nice person, for example. It is really more a social issue for the child, who would be more distanced from his friends if he did not participate. It is a good decision on the part of the parent. Later, as he gets to be eight or nine years old and can understand his own level of skill and how much he enjoys the activity, he should be allowed to decide if he wants to participate.

Responsibility for Being Happy

One day I saw two sisters—age eight and ten—for a checkup, and we started chatting about their family. They were lively, talkative, and full of life. When I asked how they got along with their big brother, they looked at each other and then their mother. It was easy to see that this was a touchy subject. Well, their mother started, "he is a little difficult and hard on the girls".

"What does he do?" I asked the girls.

"Nothing really bad to us," they responded, "but he just never likes what we want to do. So we usually end up doing what he wants to do."

"Even, when it's your turn to pick something?"

"Yeah, it's better than having him mope and complain all night, and it's usually something that we can enjoy too."

This situation often happens with the first child because the parents have taken complete responsibility for making this child happy, instead of just making it possible for him to be happy. There are a lot of things that you want for your child, but you cannot make everything happen for your child. Making sure they have a good time and smile is one of those things. We can only make it possible for him to have a good time and smile.

Given an unfamiliar situation, some shy children want the parent to be responsible for making sure that they have a good time, and they will keep expecting that of the parent as long as the parent allows it to be her responsibility. The same principle is at work in the scenario described above. The difference is that these parents have shifted part of the responsibility for their son's happiness to their daughters. They did not really do that on purpose, but it has happened nonetheless, because the parents could never seem to satisfy this child's emotional needs. Eventually they had allowed their son's moodiness to control the family's social life.

When this mother looked at the situation with wide opened eyes, she decided it was only fair that the girls get their choice, and that it was her responsibility to support her girls. It is up to their brother to smile and enjoy life, not anyone else. The mother reported that they made the transition (not easily), and that they were all happier. While it may seem like the sisters are best served by this change, it is actually the older brother, who would not continue to use a negative attitude to get his way..

The Siblings

The arrival of the second child in a family starts a chorus of advice and opinions that is only surpassed by the advice that cascaded in when the mother announced she was pregnant for the first time. In both cases, all the old clichés are dusted off and dispensed as gems of wisdom. Unfortunately, much of the advice is outdated or even wrong. Amazingly, many are worst-case-scenario stories. The feel-good story is told less often.

Jealous of The New Baby?

What is often said to parents expecting their second child is that the first will be jealous and want to send the baby back. Another parent might point out that when she picked up her new baby, her first child acted jealous. But, is it really jealousy, or that she saw her mother pick up another child and decided she would like to be picked up as well, not instead of, the other child? If the mother had another set of arms, there would not be a problem.

Jealousy is not really possible at this age because the toddler is too young to have the abstract thinking required to produce jealousy. But, the parent reports that the older child is upset and acting out more than usual. The problem to him is simply that his mother is not paying attention to his needs, not that she is holding another baby. She could care less that the mother is busy with the baby; she wants his mother now!

A different situation might help illustrate this point. For example, say you are getting ready for a big party and too busy to play with your child. She starts acting out in the same way as when you were busy with the baby, but we would not say it is because she is jealous of parties. We would know that she was upset with us for putting her off. As a toddler she is still too immature to give her busy mother's needs any consideration whether it is a new baby or preparations for a party..

It is important to be clear that she is not really jealous for two reasons. First, when we think our child is being jealous, we are assigning her a negative characteristic. Second, if we try to prevent her from being jealous, will we succeed when she isn't really jealous in the first place? It is more likely that we will be even more frustrated that all our efforts at giving her "special" time and favors are not working or appreciated.

If the mother realizes that the real issue is that she, by herself, has too much to do, then she can be proactive and plan a better strategy. A simple step would be to engage the child in an activity that generally occupies her before she settles in with the baby, and have a good back-up plan that she can easily implement while she is caring for the baby. Hiring a young neighbor to come and be a mother's helper and just play with the older child is another good possibility.

Another thing that some parents point out as "jealous" behavior is when an older sibling pokes the baby and makes her cry. Most of this behavior is not malicious, but rather comes from curiosity. The older child wants to see if she can make the baby "do something," or maybe she is just being heavy handed when she handles the baby. We would not let her near anything else that is valuable and fragile, but the baby is a different situation because we want our older child to have a relationship and be engaged with the baby. When something happens, then some parents see that as proof that she is jealous and trying to hurt the baby. But, again, think about it in a different context: If she broke a beautiful and expensive crystal vase, we would not say she was jealous of the vase, and if we are fair, we might even be more upset with ourselves that we left it within her reach without our supervision.

The same goes for the baby, we need to be sure that the baby is safe from harm. It is a good idea to put the baby in a room that can be locked when he is put down for a nap, so that the toddler will not have access to the sleeping baby. It is the same principle as locking up medicines, toxic materials, or valuable items so that they are safely out of reach when you are not around. You can also talk about being gentle with the baby, but your toddler is still too young for you to expect that she will consistently.do what you are trying to teach her.

New Conflict Between the Baby and the Toddler

Many parents note that surprisingly, the toddler seemed to enjoy her younger sibling in the first eight months or so, but now problems are occurring. The first eight months go smoothly for the toddler because it is her prerogative whether she and the baby interact or not. But, at around eight months, the baby becomes mobile and starts to initiate interaction, too. Then the conflicts begin (just as they did with you and your first child). Now the baby is grabbing the toys and knocking down what her older sibling has been playing with.

The usual response by the parent is to put the burden of making their relationship work on the toddler. Comments from the parent range from "let him have that," and "you have so many toys," to "he is just a baby," "give it to him now," or "you need to learn to share." The two- or three-year-old is just not mature enough to do these things willingly. She does not have a clue about being altruistic or sharing, but the parent still demands better behavior from her simply because she is older, and she sees these moments as "teaching opportunities." As discussed before, often these teaching sessions are in reality demands for compliance.

A better approach for the parent is to take it upon herself to make it work for both kids. Just as we have this tradition to punish every misstep, we always seem to want to teach the child a lesson in these instances, particularly when sharing is the topic. At this age and even a little older, it is usually better to forgo the "teaching moment" and just help both kids be happy. As we discussed before, the toddler is still too young to digest and store this as a lesson to remember for life.

Making them happy in the moment adds up over time and they learn in a positive way about having fun and getting along together. They learn that they do not need to cry and get upset to resolve every problem. As they get older we can offer choices and suggestions for how to compromise and share better. As they gain more awareness, they see that they have more fun together because they share and look out for each other. It all starts with the parents not letting the early conflicts escalate.

Helping Our Children Deal with Each Other

Helping our children become best friends is one of the most important duties of parenting. Parents need to be alert to mean behavior and teasing, which can fly below the parent's radar. Parents are quick to stop physical aggressiveness but, are often tuned out or lackadaisical about verbal or psychological attacks. The latter is often what the older child does to their younger sibling because they are well aware of the parent's rapid and strong response to physical attacks.

In my office I have seen siblings acting out and annoying each other (not to mention me), while the parent calmly sat and did nothing to rectify the situation. After I intervened, I asked don't you stop this bickering between your children? The answer was, "My brother and I did that when we were growing up too." And then in a matter of fact manner tone, "Yeah, we didn't like each other much. In fact, we rarely have much to do with each other now." How does one view this state of affairs as acceptable? Accepting the loss of the love and unconditional support that only comes from "family" in such a matter-of-fact way is tragic.

Many parents carry memories of unpleasant encounters during their formative years with their own parents and siblings. These experiences can lead to lasting resentments between parents and children and between siblings, and can disrupt family life for generations to come. I have encountered more parents than I would have expected who have had little or nothing to do with a sibling or a parent after they left home.

This state of estrangement is bad enough, but because they did not receive the wisdom and guidance their own parents could have given them in their formative years, they now do not have all of the tools they need for parenting their own children. They come from families who settled for an "okay" relationship, and so they bring that perspective into their own families. Instead of striving for the best, they play to low expectations that they feel are "normal" for any family.

A mother once came to see me because she had finally realized that her teenagers were displaying real anger towards each other. I had seen all of the family throughout the years, and individually, they all seemed nice and likeable. The mother was aware of friction between them, but attributed it to kids being kids. She did not even take it seriously when her daughter's friends told her how openly mean they were to each other at school, calling out insults as they passed in the halls.

She finally came in one day because she heard the older brother laughing at his sister after zinging her with a nasty remark. As he turned away laughing, she saw her daughter jump on his back and start clawing into his face. It was finally clear to her that it was not just a harmless case of "kids being kids" and that they would grow out of it. This was the culmination of many nasty verbal encounters that the parents barely noted and thought little of. Even with the parents now clear on the harm being done, it's not clear that these siblings would ever be friends.

Young children will have many clashes as they grow up together. In the toddler years their behavioral abilities are minimal and they are not capable of compromising and settling their disputes. If the parent does nothing to bring harmony to the situation, the bickering and fighting will become their way of handling conflict. Some parents stop them only when the commotion is so loud that it annoys them. It is crucial that parents take proactive steps to stop the fighting and teach them how to settle their differences in a more positive way.

Positioning our children to enjoy us and each other is one of the most important tasks of parents. It is not a matter of luck to have great kids; it is a product of watchful parents who are proactive in all of the interactions of the family. For most of the time that a family lives together the parents are the leaders who can set the stage for the happiness of everyone. There is no greater and long-lasting gift that your children can inherit from you than a close and loving relationship with their siblings.

Another Side of Aggressive Behavior

A mother came in one day, very distraught about her son. She told me that she was helping out at his kindergarten class, and saw a much smaller girl come up to him, shove him, and grab what he had in his hand. He did nothing to stop her and just cried. Other similar things happened while she was there, and she also noticed that he did not try to answer questions that she was sure he knew.

The problem is that a good principle—not hitting others—was taken too seriously at too young an age. When young children have conflict with each other at one to three years, they are developmentally likely to push, shove, hit, and even bite; not "use their words". If we do not allow this behavior to a reasonable degree, we can take away all of their aggressive behavior, even those that are positive. Like the big kindergartener they will not defend themselves when bothered by their playmates because they have learned to fear the wrath of their well-meaning, but overzealous parent, and simply let the other children have their way with them.

If you look around at other children you will see that most two-year-olds tend to be physical when they have conflict with their peers, while five-year-olds are mostly using their words. Some parents believe that all their sternness and threats have worked and that is why their five-year-old does not hit anymore. The reality is that they have matured developmentally and as five-year-olds can handle these conflicts and stand up for themselves in a verbal way.

An unintended consequence of automatically stifling all physically aggressive behavior at one to two is that it can affect other aggressive behaviors that are later seen as being positive. A two-year-old child's aggressiveness towards the outside world is generally physical, and will later become more diversified in its expression and more socially acceptable. Raising your hand in class, defending yourself, and wanting to compete are all aggressive acts that may be poorly developed if the child's first aggressive acts (being physical with other children) were always stopped and even punished without regard for the whole context of what happened. As in most things in life, balance is a good thing.

One of our daughters' friends commented on how close she seemed to be to her brother and sister. She wanted to know what we had done to encourage this. There are, of course, many factors involved, but I feel that one important strategy was that we always stopped mean behavior between them. When they were very young, we simply stepped in and stopped the problem and corrected it for all of them. We tried to get them out of each other's faces and figure out something that worked for all of them without scolding and long lectures.

Later, when they could understand better, we would tell them there were three ways you could act towards your brother or sister: You could say something nice, neutral, or mean. But, in our family, "mean" was not an option. We could not make them say something nice, but we would intervene if we heard them say anything mean. There were a lot of protests to this edict in the form of, "What about when he or she does…?" Our answer was, "Try to settle it without being mean or say nothing at all. If it seems to be a huge unsolvable problem, let us help."

Summary

- Raising the first child is a learning experience
- Jealousy is not really the issue in the toddler-baby relationship
- Sibling rivalry is not a normal, unavoidable event
- Parents have the responsibility, the ability, and the duty to prevent sibling rivalry
- One of the most important goals of your parenting is to help your children to be best friends
- Aggressive behavior can be positive
- Yes, parents have too much to do to be perfect.

CHAPTER 13: THINKING OUTSIDE OF THE BOX

You can't lead the people if you don't love the people. You can't save the people if you don't serve the people.

-   Cornel West

When I was a teenager learning to drive, I thought that my hotshot driving showed how skillful I was. My father commented that I was only as good a driver as my passengers were comfortable. At the time I didn't pay any attention to his logic, but as I got older and experienced rough and uncomfortable rides with others myself, I came to take his advice to heart.

Later, in thinking about parenting, it seemed to be the perfect analogy for parents. The parent has primary control of this journey through life, and while he is negotiating the bumps and curves, he needs to consider the comfort of his passengers, his children. Clearly the parent is in charge of the general path and direction they take, but are his passengers happy and enjoying the ride? With all your powers as the parent, comes the responsibility to look after the needs of those whom you are directing. This has been expressed by many philosophers in the past.

From Cynthia Brown's book "Big History", she writes, "a few years later, John Locke, too, defended the rights of parliament against the rights of a monarch in 'Two Treatises of Government' (1690). In these essays Locke argued that men submit to government, not because the inclination to submit to an absolute leader is innately present in people, but because legitimate government protects their right to property. If government doesn't offer this protection, then men of wealth have a right to withdraw their consent to government and to form a new one. Kings have no right to rule, but rather men have a right to consent."

To strengthen his case, Locke developed a new theory of mind, in which he denied there were any innate ideas, including the inclination to submit to absolute authority. On the contrary, Locke argued, the mind of a newborn is a tabula rasa, or blank slate, into which all ideas come from experience and reason.

Menicus, a Chinese philosopher of the Confuscian school, argued that it is acceptable for the subjects to overthrow and even kill (a little strong for our discussion) a ruler who ignores the people's needs and rules harshly. He believed in the innate moral goodness of all human beings, and "proclaimed that "all babies who are smiled at and hugged will know how to love'." He and the western philosopher Plato agreed in the innate moral goodness of all human beings.

Deming

My favorite source of outside the box thinking in the context of parenting is W. Edward Deming who is credited with helping Japanese industry to reemerge after WWII, by teaching them his guidelines for business. Part of his advice was to interview and hire people and place them in positions that suited their abilities, and then help them to succeed. He felt that if the worker was not doing well, it was a system failure and that it was the responsibility of management to correct the system or place the worker in a more suitable position.

How Deming's Ideas Are Relevant to Good Parenting

His points in transforming people in the work place were as follows:

- Set an example (model and mentor)
- Be a good listener, but do not compromise your principles (be open to other opinions, but stay with your beliefs)
- Continually teach other people (teach change, not demand change)
- Help people to pull away from their current practices and beliefs and move into the new philosophy without a feeling of guilt about the past (shaming and criticism are not necessary to move forward)

Deming's principles for business had extraordinary success in Japan, were he was honored, and later in the USA. It shows the value of good management and leadership where those in power (parents) take the responsibility for making the system work and helping their employees (children) succeed. If you just take away the above four points Deming used in industry and practiced them with your children you would have the essence of proactive parenting and the practice of teaching and mentoring. Dr. Deming's ideas can be found in more detail on the internet and in his books.

Summerhill

Summerhill is a boarding school started by A.S. Neill. Its underlying philosophy was that the school should let the child's developmental stage and interests guide him. The children should have access to quality educators but should have the power to decide what they want to study, not what the adults, neither teachers nor parents, thought was best. Initially the children had an equal voice in all affairs of the school, but it soon became apparent to Neill and his teachers that issues of safety and finance needed to be supervised by the adults.

You might not be surprised that the "hippies" embraced his ideas in the 1960's, but you may be more surprised that this school actually started in Great Britain in 1921. He reported that his students were generally successful and were accepted at Cambridge and Oxford as well as other elite colleges. He was equally proud that a frequent comment was that his students stood out as "good people". This was attributed to the fact that the school served each individual child as its starting point, not the child fulfilling the demands of the school. Their self-esteem was always supported and nurtured.

In each of these examples whether the person in charge

is a king or the driver of a car or a businessman, the argument is that the authority figure has more responsibility to do the right thing than the less powerful has the duty to submit mindlessly. Does this mean that the child is totally in charge? Certainly not, but it does emphasize that parents must try to see the child's needs as being as important to consider as their own.   .

The opinion of these philosophers and other leaders is that we must pay attention to the needs of those whom we are leading. Parents can see the big picture better if they consider their children's point of view. If the parent is open to looking at all sides of a dispute they will find good solutions. The parent should think in a more proactive way and teach and mentor rather than just demand compliance from their child.

Are You Trying to Help Your Child to Grow and Succeed in Life, or Is It More Important to You That They Follow Your Rules and Obey You?

Many schools are now finding success in reducing suspensions of children by helping them to adapt to their situation. Part of this change came when the problem was restated as how do we help the children to stay in school, rather than for what offenses do we kick them out. Looking at the problem from the children's point of view, rather than the teacher's need for discipline made all the difference to finding good solutions. The ends were essentially the same, but the means made all the difference.

The "No child left behind" legislation was criticized for some of its methods. While there are many well intentioned points in the law, one flaw was that it treated the schools and teachers in the same   negative way that problem children were treated, with the threat of punishment if standards were not met rather than emphasizing help and more resources for system failures in difficult situations. Just as with our own children, these methods crush morale and inspire deceptive behavior.

These thinkers from other disciplines are referencing the principles of the Golden Rule; "do unto others as you would have others do unto you." Almost all of the world's major religions have some form of this as a cornerstone of their religious philosophy. It is a way of acting toward others in general, religious or secular. It should be a "no-brainer" to apply this to parenting our children, but the traditions of Parenting 101 dictate a demanding adversarial path.

In the next section we will look at the factors that keep parents from doing unto their children as they would others, especially adults.

CHAPTER 14: WHY THREATS AND PUNISHMENT DO NOT WORK

I've learned that people will forgive what you said, people will forget what you did, but people will never forget how you made them feel.

- Maya Angelou

Punishment's Changing History

The evolution of punishments is an interesting subject in itself. For many of us it starts with the legendary horror stories of some great grandpa who used a big leather belt and left scars on his children. The next generation had hard hand spanking on bare bottoms as a standard, and then the next generation only spanked on the diaper to avoid real injury. Then corporeal punishment, in general, was questioned. There are still debates about corporeal punishments in the home and even in the schools, but more are seeing it as unreasonable. Currently, a privilege will be taken away or there will be a time out. This softening of harsh punishments suggests a societal sense that there must be better ways to limit their children's behavior. Or is it that parents were having a hard time thinking of times when they would accept being hit by their boss?

At the same time this change from physical punishment to psychological or verbal punishment has created a perception problem for parents. It was easy to realize that they were punishing their child when they spanked him, and often parents tried to apologize for having to do something that they did not like to do They expressed their ambiguity by saying "this hurts me more than it hurts you." "Seriously? Bend over, Dad!"

With our current trend to more verbal disapproval or punishment, many parents do not see as clearly the impact of their methods as a cause of anger and ill feelings and loss of self-esteem in their children. The child feels this psychological disapproval and rejection just as deeply as any physical punishment. The techniques of punishing have changed, but it is still the same process of intimidation and alienation to the child.

Does the Punishment Fit the Crime?

The traditional punishment system of Parenting 101 often lacks a correlation between the crime and the punishment. The punishment may be taking away something that the parent knows her child values, but has nothing to do with the crime. For example, if your son hits his sister, is taking away a TV program going to make the point, or would no dessert be better? If you make a mistake at work, what would be more appropriate, no lunch break or no texting?

Simply punishing the child as a way of changing behavior has an affect on some children, but for the wrong reasons. In a conflict the choice for the child becomes satisfy his anger and hit his sister, or protect something that he doesn't want taken away. This dilemma will continue for the child if the parent has not taught him better ways to prevent or resolve the problem. Even a discussion about better solutions can be obscured by anger over the punishment. As the child gets older he looks at the punishment as having no relevance and questions its validity and yours

The Endless Path of Crime and Punishments

Parents resort to threats and punishments to maintain discipline because they feel that explaining in a nice way gets them nowhere, and that threatening or punishing their child is the only way to get her to obey. But, were your methods really thoughtful? Did you not yell, but still glared and showed your displeasure in your body language?

What some parents are not seeing clearly is that they are asking more of their child than she can deliver at her young age. The failure to comply by the child is not viewed as immaturity, but as stubbornness. Tradition has taught the parents that they no choice but to use punishments to get compliance. But, as the next story shows, while punishments may instill better behavior temporarily, an endless cycle may ensue.

Yes, This Is a True Story

A couple asked for my advice on how to get their 17-year-old daughter to be less rude to them. They said that she used crude language with them and called them all kinds of derogatory names. "What have you tried to do about this," I asked rather incredulously. They replied that they had been able to get her to stop in the last year because she was the oldest of her friends and the only one who drove, so they said she could only use the car if she cleaned up her language. It worked until more of her friends could drive, and then she went back to using crude language. They were at a loss as to what punishment they could hold over her next.

This is an unfortunate example of the endless path that using consequences and punishments can take. At first, they took something away that they thought was important to the child. No dessert, no bed time story, no TV. As she got older, she lost privileges and allowances. It finally culminated in not being able to use the car. What happens when you run out of consequences and punishments?

These kind and caring parents had bought into Parenting 101's crime and punishment method of raising their child. It led them to believe that simply giving consequences for unacceptable behavior was all that was needed to make their child do the right thing. There may have been some teaching but the emphasis was on using punishment as a deterrent for bad behavior. This approach made punishment the central issue to the child, not whether what she was doing was right or wrong.

It is easy to imagine that these parents would have embraced a more child-friendly approach of stopping bad behavior. But, it is hard to overcome tradition and the societal norm, and look for other approaches, when they are stuck in a cycle of looking for more effective punishments.

Consequences

Imagine that a teenager is in a situation where his friends want to do something that he clearly knows is outside his family's rules. If he has been raised by a crime and punishment method, is it possible that his thought process will be as follows? "I know my parents will be mad if I do this, but I probably won't be caught, and besides I can deal with the punishment." There isn't any thought given to the right or wrong of the issue in the teenager's mind, only, can I get away with this. There has been little positive teaching of how to handle the situation in the future.

In contrast, a mother related to me that she wanted to raise her children in the manner that her husband was. She had been raised in a house of strict discipline and punishments. She related how her brother-in-law was asked by his wild and crazy friends why he was such a straight arrow. His reply was that his dad had raised him and his brother as a single parent, and had always treated them with respect and taught them to do the right thing rather than threaten them, and that when they had a problem he was always there to help them. That was why he felt that he couldn't disrespect his father's standards just to have a little more so-called fun.

The greatest damage of this crime and punishment system is to the child's self-esteem. Feeling disappointment and anger from the one you depend upon and love the most erodes it. Self-esteem underlies every part of our child's successful journey through life. Parents need to meet the challenge of learning to instill and preserve it in their child, while positioning their child to become a good and productive adult. No pampering parents and out of control kids need apply here

In the end the crime and punishment scenario settles for half the job. If the child complies only out of fear of punishment you have a partial and temporary fix. They will follow the rules as long as the punishment deters them. If they don't care about the punishment (something taken away no longer matters to them) there is no longer a reason to do what the parents feel is right. The lesson of how to do the right thing has never been given or emphasized. Doing the right thing is replaced by avoiding a punishment.

The use of anger and shaming to emphasize your point only serves to further erode your child's self-esteem and resilience

Summary

- Disciplining comes from expecting a child to have behaviors that are beyond their developmental level and finding that explaining is not working.
- Punishing children to get compliance is a long held practice.
- Punishments create anger and get cooperation only because of fear rather than understanding.
- The unfairness of the punishment may become the main issue to the child, rather than the issue that needs correcting
- An unintended consequence of punishments is that the child tries to avoid them by becoming secretive and does not seek help with controversial problems from their parents.
- Do not let disciplining and punishing erode your child's self-esteem.

CHAPTER 15: ANOTHER LOOK AT COMPLIANCE, RESPECT, AND OTHER VIRTUES

I always find it more difficult to say things I mean than the things I don't.

- W. Somerset Maugham
  The Painted Veil

Children must be taught to think, not what to think.

- Margaret Mead

The principles of Parenting 101 are based on compliance, respect, and virtues. The problem is that these terms have become important in and of themselves, and obscure what parents should really be trying proactively to instill in their children; how to become a good and productive person.

Compliance

Parents want their child to learn to do things in an approved way, but their emphasis on compliance often misses the point. As an example, a mother wants her child to eat a balanced healthy diet, but if he refuses to eat what she offers, she begins to use coercion. Her comments often take an adversarial, demanding tone: "You will eat that," or "you will sit there until you try everything," or the ever popular "there will be no dessert unless you finish that."

The mother started by trying to get her child to eat in a healthy way. But soon her main goal is that he complies and obeys her. If she is trying, out of our concern for his health, to get her child to eat a good diet, why is she now threatening him? Without realizing it, she has changed her focus of helping him to eat well, to making him obey her demands to eat what she has put on his plate.

The need for compliance comes from a traditional belief that when parents ask or order their child to do something, the child should or must do whatever is asked of him. This paradigm is steeped in the tradition of many generations of Parenting 101. It goes back to our discussion of the style of parenting that put the parent in an unquestioned position of authority. Not only did the parent have this position of absolute authority over their child, their peers expected them to exercise it. What is even more destructive is that even if the parent realizes later that she has been unfair, she sticks to her guns for fear of eroding her position of authority.

Winning compliance by force and threats does not accomplish anything positive for the future, instead often creates more bad feelings. Being willing to debate an issue with your child or even, on reflection, being willing to admit you are wrong, shows your confidence in yourself as a mentor for your child. You do not have to win every conflict to know that you are a good and strong parent. These conflicts shouldn't be about the parent always coming out on top by demanding compliance, they should be about finding mutually satisfying solutions.

On the other hand it is important to point out that some situations do not require a lot of discussion or give and take. As with the example of the knife or something as obviously dangerous, it is up to the parent to speak in simple declarative sentences and put the knife somewhere safe. When the situation is obvious to us, we tend to act objectively without the need for threats and consequences. We let our actions speak for themselves. We act pragmatically and do not make it an issue of compliance.

Respect

Respect for the authority of the parent is a long-standing tradition. It is as if it is not enough for the child to do the right thing; first there must be some acknowledgement of the supremacy of the parent. Over the years, this position has softened, but it has not gone away completely. When parents are in a confrontation with their child and he continues to resist, some parents will fall back on "because I'm your parent and I said so", or "and you will respect me". Respect of the parent becomes more important than a job well done.

Respect is closely associated with compliance. When parents demand respect they require compliance. When a child complies with the threats and demands of an angry parent it is not respect, but fear. Earning respect is not a one way street, it needs to flow in both directions.

It Should, in Fact, Start From the Parent's Side

A young child needs to experience respectful behavior in order to learn it, and as he gets older can learn more from thoughtful discussions about it. A child raised in an authoritarian setting may not experience respect or reasoning; he only learns to fear his parents' anger if he does not comply. Given and shown many examples of respect, the child will learn and reciprocate the respect shown him in due time.

Sharing

Virtues, like honesty and sharing, are so highly valued that we try to teach them to our children whenever they come up, regardless of their age or ability to understand the lesson. Two- and three-year-olds are often scolded for not sharing because the parent thinks it is such an important virtue. But, most developmentalists would say that sharing is only beginning, not accomplished, at three.

Instead of lecturing bickering toddlers on the principles of how to share, at first, the parent should just step in and figure out how to help make it possible for everyone to be happy. When the interventions are calm and fair, children will start to learn more from the modeling of the parent, not the lectures and demands.

Even when we have managed to make our child give up something to our glaring friend's crying child, it will still happen again and again until his developmental stage allows him to handle the situation. Making the moment work should be your goal, not teaching a life lesson in sharing at this young age. You are the person most capable of making the situation work and finding the best compromise. So take charge and do it.

Every time you fix the moment, you are modelling and teaching the children about playing together and sharing. Your children will more readily adopt your methods when they are friendly and helpful. It takes many steps, but it will come in a much more pleasant way than by multiple confrontations and demands, and then meltdowns. There is not a sudden change. Remember the thermometer graph metaphor. Progress is being made, things are getting better; it just takes time to reach your goal of behavioral maturity.

Honesty

The mother of a five-year-old came to ask me for help in dealing with her son's dishonesty. He came home one day after playing with his friend Joey and started playing with a shiny new toy car on the kitchen table. She asked where the car had come from and he said his friend had given it to him. Then she started asking leading questions, hoping that he would voluntarily confess his sins. He insisted that his friend had given it to him, and she blew up, saying, "I know that you took it and that is stealing and I'm ashamed of you. I'm driving you back to their house and you are going to return the car and apologize." On the way home, she continued to express her disappointment in him, and warned him that his punishment would be much worse if she "caught him stealing again".

Three weeks later she was cleaning his bedroom, and to her horror she found another car that he had hidden under his mattress. She felt that all her efforts to teach him to be honest had not only failed, but he had also become sneaky. I asked her what she felt she had taught him the first time.

She soon realized that she just wanted him to confess, and had not addressed the real issue: how to properly get something he desired. In fact, when she questioned him she was being deceptive too, because she was acting like she had no idea that he had taken the car without his friend's knowledge.

She could have immediately stated that they needed to return the car to his friend because it was not appropriate for his friend to have given it to him. The car ride to the friend's house would have been a good time to talk about acceptable ways to get something he wants. He could have come to her and told her that he wanted a car like his friend's. She could have suggested an upcoming birthday or holiday or given him a little job so that he could earn money to buy it himself.

Discussing "honesty" as a concept at this age has limited impact because he does not have the abstract thinking he needs to help him understand all of the issues. Like a lot of problems brought up at this early age parents are focusing on the wrong part of the issue because it involves a virtue that she wants her child to have for the rest of his life. But, this should not have been about honesty; it should have been about getting things that you want in a way that is acceptable to your parents. As your child matures, learning to do things in an appropriate way becomes the basis for his honesty.

The immediate unintended consequence of her punitive approach was that he became sneaky. The only part of his mother's advice that he tried to follow was "don't let me catch you doing this again." Another possible negative consequence is that he might start to feel that it is not always a good idea to talk to his parents about controversial issues. He feels that they will get angry and/or punitive if he brings them up.

Again, the problem for parents is that they are not clear on their child's skill sets. The need for instilling a virtue overrides being clear about what the child is actually developmentally capable of doing, and threats are used instead of instruction. The parent is putting compliance ahead of the basic issue of how to do things in an acceptable manner.

Resilience

Resilience is being discussed as an alternative or reaction to the helicopter parenting that seems to be prevalent these days. Some have suggested that our children need to be put in situations that are difficult and be allowed to figure them out by themselves and be allowed to fail at times. Having these occasional negative results is supposed to lead them to have resilience.

It still is a negative approach like many old traditions of parenting. As in the honesty issue, the test or exam is given to the child without a first step of prior preparation or study. When these issues come up, the parent's emphasis on their child doing the right thing leads them to skip over the fact that their child has not been prepared to handle the test.

These tests in life are just like school tests, we do better when we had been taught and learned the material before the test is given. The self confidence that is needed to handle adversity is taught up by the parent over time. Proactive teaching and mentoring of your child will help prepare her to have the self-esteem and confidence to succeed, and the resilience to risk failure.

We need to reconsider what the teaching of compliance, respect, and virtues is all about. These areas of parenting have taken on a life of their own. Demanding that all parental orders be obeyed to please the parent should be replaced by the parent understanding the child's developmental abilities better with the goal of proactively helping the child to progress and succeed with self-confidence and resilience. All of the virtues need to be modeled, mentored and taught, not just demanded of your child.

Summary

- Traditional parenting has made compliance, obedience, and respect more important to parents than the lessons that they are trying to impart
- Compliance as an end in itself should be replaced with a mutual solving of problems and reaching a common goal.
- Respects starts with the parent respecting their child's feelings and needs,
- Children will return respect once their abstract thinking kicks in and they realize that they have such great parents
- Respect and other virtues are built slowly, one step at a time.

Raise your child in a positive way without the need to shame or punish, find a way that both you and your child enjoy and that fosters their self-esteem and builds their trust in you. Be your child's best friend and support and resource forever.

- Your child knows that you will always help them
- Even in the hardest moments he feels your love

- You make him feel good about himself

CHAPTER 16: TEACHING GOOD BEHAVIOR, NOT JUST SETTING LIMITS

I know one thing – the negative way of teaching for me, it never worked.

- Joe Madden, Manager of the Tampa Bay Rays and Chicago Cubs

Parents see setting limits as one of their main job. They feel that their principles are too important to back away from, and that punishments are sometimes necessary. But, look at this in another way, teaching good behavior reaches the same goal, but in a positive way.

Parents are positioned by tradition (parenting 101) to engage their child in a confrontational manner, threatening punishments if their child doesn't stay within the family limits. Without backing away from your principles, it can be a positive learning experience rather than an adversarial event. The image should be of you and your child sitting on the same side of the table, figuring out how to solve a problem together. Not one of sitting across the table glaring at each other in a confrontational atmosphere.

Friendly sessions can lead to good solutions if the child feels that they are equal participants, and that the solutions are not always going the parent's way. The proactive approach again helps to open doors to alternative positive possibilities rather than just closing doors to unacceptable behaviors.

Early on, at two and three, limit setting by threats doesn't work well because the child's behavioral development is not mature enough. Rather than trying to make our child fit into a system that requires the ability to reason and understand, the parent can proactively act to avoid situations that don't match their child's developmental abilities. We can't do this forever, but it is appropriate for more than the first several years of your child's life. Soon our requests will be met by a more mature and understanding child. At the same time the child will accept guidelines given in a repetitive and friendly way even though they may not fully understand it. "It's what we do in our family."

The Metaphorical Fence

You have a back yard with a neighbor's unfenced pool on one side, a threatening dog on another, and a beautiful garden on the third side; and your toddler keeps heading for one danger or the other. It seems that no matter how much you explain, yell, or punish, your toddler does not listen. What can you do and say? Instead of saying anything, change the situation. In this case just build a fence around your property.

The fence prevents the child from harming herself and other people's property without arguing, yelling, or punishing. The fence sets the limits that we want without harshness or anger, in fact, without any commentary. Your toddler has not really learned anything, but at this point in her life we are primarily interested in her safety and protecting our neighbor's garden. Without the fence, you resort to threats and punishments because you do not have a convenient solution.

As a parent you can be the metaphorical fence that safeguards your child without threats or punishments until she is mature enough to learn better solutions from you or understand how to avoid problems on her own.

The Amazing Fence

- A fence clearly defines the limits
- A fence is immediate and pragmatic
- A fence does not demean by punishing, threatening, or shaming
- A fence is consistent and constant
- A fence does not waver in the face of pleading and angry remarks

Becoming the Fence

When your child begins to understand your reasoning and explanations, you can discuss the reasons for your limits and restriction, and then give him ways to work within the boundaries that you think are safe and appropriate. When does this occur? A little understanding and cooperation appear at three or four, but think again of when you would allow your child to walk to school by himself, or handle a knife, or have more than a dollar in his pocket. In some cases it is at five or six, but even closer to eight years old.

In the fence analogy, the limits are physically set without comment, good or bad. The fence simply limits bad or dangerous behavior by its presence alone. The quicker and more persistently you act, the better. And remember you do not need to be harsh or threatening; it is unnecessary, ineffective, and actually counter-productive. Your quick and persistent actions show the child that you will not change your mind, any more than a fence would.

The difference between the fence and the parent is that the fence cannot be affected by pushback. For various reasons and to various degrees, pushback affects parents. Parents are all too human and loud screaming and sad puppy dog eyes have their effect.

Some parents feel that it is not possible to always resist their high-spirited child, but, I can recall very few, if any, parents telling me that they had a child who persistently posed a problem of running at a busy street corner. The parent's concern for the safety of their child automatically appears in their actions, words, and body language in this situation and convinces the child that being uncooperative is not an option. You have instinctively become the metaphorical fence and after a few attempts he behaves in a cooperative way. But, don't let go of his hand, just yet!

It is beneficial to you to act as decisively, firmly, and quickly in other less dangerous or less important situations. They may not be dangerous, but they make up for it in being frustrating and annoying.

Is it futile to say "no" until your child can reason and understand? No, it is not. In fact, much of what they learn in terms of limitation to their behavior is by rote, rather than reason. Saying no to a multitude of circumstances is necessary, and at the same time not always explainable to a toddler. But, the repetition of the limit, the no, in a prompt, firm, friendly, and consistent way will start to get some compliance. The child sees you as an unyielding fence. A mother once told me that she thought she was getting nowhere with a certain rule with her child, and then overheard her child admonishing a playmate with the rule that she had been trying to get her child to follow, in an uncanny imitation of the mother.

Setting limits starts with learning how to say "no" in a friendly but convincing way. This means that you have learned how to act effectively in stopping and changing behavior that you do not approve of. Often parents will not limit bad behavior because they do not want to be as harsh as they remember their own parents. They mistakenly believe that harshness is the only way to stop bad behavior, and so they present a wishy-washy stance that the child does not heed. This behavior by the parent actually invites more resistance, temper tantrums, and meltdowns over trivial issues.

This was illustrated beautifully in the comic strip, For Better or Worse, where a worried child asks his friend why they haven't stopped what they were doing, like his mother has been telling them. The son replies, because "she hasn't yelled yet". Over his short lifetime this child has learned that the real signal to listen for is not her first or even third or fourth request, but when she final loses her temper and starts yelling. Understandably, the harried mother would like to be able to direct her child without having to drop what she is doing. What she is not taking into account is that her child has learned to react to her signals, more than her words.

The mother needs to do something that is definite, immediate, and effective. This requires that she position herself to do all of the above. She does not have the convenience that the fence has of limiting a given area. She should take the extra ten seconds to walk over, put her hand on his shoulder, and say in a firm and kind voice, "I need to have you do this now." This will be much more effective. After the child gets used to this procedure, he will start to respond like Pavlov's dog to the sound of her bell-like voice.

We have a parental duty to limit socially unacceptable behavior whatever the age of the child, and then spend the time to teach better behaviors. It benefits the rest of us, but most importantly, it benefits the parents and the child. Do it without resorting to the old harsh and punitive techniques that I have been arguing against. Above all, try to maintain a sense of humor. Engage your child like she's the person you love the most.

Pragmatism

Adding pragmatism as a factor in your initial thinking and actions helps. As an example, is it really necessary to wait until your child is not protesting to change her diaper? I do not think so. If you have little tricks that smooth the way in a few seconds, they are well worth using. But, if it is going to take even a few minutes it is becoming a waste of your time. And worse, your procrastinating encourages more protesting on the child's part. Putting off what you clearly must do, is an invitation to the child to continue to protest.

Putting the child in their seat belt is another example of an area that is so repetitive in the life of the parent and child that allowing it to degenerate into minutes-long crying struggles is more than any parents should inflict upon themselves and their child. These early struggles are setting a pattern that the child instinctively expands into power struggles. It is hard not to give in to your child's protests at times, but unless you have reached a good quick compromise, you are encouraging more protests.

When you are trying to resolve disruptive conflicts, make a list of these conflicts, like changing diapers, putting on seatbelts, or going to school that are most annoying and repetitive with your child, and brainstorm them with your spouse or a friend. Think of all the variables that are involved:

- Am I sure of what I want the outcome to be?
- Am I taking my child's needs into account?
- Am I clear on her developmental abilities/limitations?
- Can I change my approach and maintain my standards?
- Am I keeping my sense of humor?

Becoming sure of what you want the result to be allows you to act proactively and decisively, and present an unwavering and confident face to your child as you state your limits. Be the calm, firm, and unwavering proverbial fence.

You can be firm and effective without being harsh and threatening. Firmness requires that you act decisively and stay with your decision regardless of those sad eyes staring at you or the crying and yelling that you are so unfair. When you are clear on the issues and the factors that made you feel confident in your position, you can act decisively and calmly. Just as you do with your child at a busy street corner.

Teaching, Not Punishing

When one of my daughters was in junior high, she and several of her friends did something wrong, and they were busted. The other parents involved sat their daughters down that week, as we did with ours. At the end of our talk with our daughter, she asked how long we were going to ground her. "Why do you want to be grounded?" we asked. She said that most of her friends were being grounded for one or two weeks, and she was hoping that we would say one week because she had something she would like to do the second weekend. Again, we asked, "Why do you want to be grounded?" This time she looked puzzled, and said. "What do you mean, why do I want to be grounded?" "Well," I said, "We talked over the problem, we explained what we expected of you, and you said you were wrong, and sorry, and would never do it again. What more do your mother and I need to hear from you? I do not think that I'll believe you more if I punish you." She finally understood, and with a big smile on her face, she gave us a hug and promised to do better in the future.

In this case, we did clearly set a limit and held her to it, with no yelling or threats, and ultimately, without punishment. Instead we explained the issues and gave her alternate behaviors that would be acceptable. By this time our children had had this type of conversation many times before, and our proactive approach allowed her to listen and accept our advice.

Setting limits is an important issue to parents, but more importantly, good and appropriate behavior must be taught. The problem is that the traditional way of setting limits has the negative sense of trying to cage our child and control them with fear of consequences, rather than teaching and opening doors to better behavior.

The goal of good behavior can be reached in a more positive way, by teaching and mentoring, and clearly showing your child that you are trying to help her. Removing "setting limits" from this chapter's title would leave a better title for this topic. Setting limits is really a parental term that is the negative way of describing the positive goal of teaching good behavior.

Summary

- Show your child the right way to do things, not just limit him by threats
- Think of yourself as a fence that sets limits: definite, immediate, consistent, non- punishing,   and unwavering
- Being wishy-washy invites tantrums and meltdowns
- At times it is best to be pragmatic; every issue does not need long drawn out explanations
- Young children first learn some rules because of repetition
- If you are unclear about your goals in a given situation; brainstorm with your spouse or a friend
- Your real goal is teaching good behavior, not just setting limits and getting obedience and compliance.
- Have a sense of humor

CHAPTER 17: FOSTERING RESPONSIBILITY, NOT DEMANDING IT

Child, child do you not see? For each of us comes
a time when we must be more than what we are

- Shunryu Suzuki
  Zen Mind, Beginners Mind

Responsibility is another one of those virtues that
parents assume should appear in their child as soon as it is
asked of them. It is as if the asking of the child to be
responsible is all a parent needs to do. Like everything else
in a child's behavioral development, becoming responsible
in the adult sense takes maturation and helpful guidance by
a thoughtful parent. It needs to be taught, not simple
demanded under threat of punishment.

Fitting Responsibility to Ability

I once saw a documentary about the nomadic Mongols
taking their horses and yurts from pasture to pasture; they

set up and took down their yurts many times. Everyone had a role in doing this quickly and efficiently. The parents had the most to do and did the technical and heavy work. The older grandparents did what they physically were capable of doing, and also watched the babies. The children were given work according to their age. What was striking to me was that even the toddlers were carrying the smaller tent poles to the horses with big smiles on their faces. They were working side by side with their parents. No more was asked of them than what they could do. There wasn't yelling at or scolding of children.

It was a beautiful example of familial cooperation. It was less about making the children responsible and more about cooperation within a family. The difference is that responsibility is usual demanded of children and family cooperation comes from accepting what the child willingly contributes. They do not understand "work ethic" at this age, but a pleasant work experience can lead to more participation in the future.

On a camping and short backpacking trip with my three adult children and their spouses and their six boys (two boys per family), I had a similar experience. The grandsons were ages six to fourteen and always have a great time together. When the work of making camp and setting up the tents was begun by the parents, their boys all wanted to pitch in and help. It wasn't just that there was nothing else to do, they were enthusiastic about doing all the work and being in charge of some part of setting up camp. Just as with Mongol families, everyone did what they could and with pride showed their parents what they had done.

In our society parents want to teach their children responsibility and give them chores to do. Usually the parents have them do a simple task like putting away a few toys, and tell them they'll be back to check on them in a few minutes while they do something else. When they get back, nothing has been done and the child may have just played and made an even bigger mess, much to the parent's displeasure. There really hasn't been much role modelling or guidance given, just an expectation that the chore was easy enough to do. Physically it was, but behaviorally to do a simple task perfectly by themselves may still be months or even years away.

Teenagers are developmentally able to cooperate and perform chores, but their resistance may have started with their parent's adversarial disciplinary approach over the years. A pattern of confrontation and conflict becomes established and full blown in our teenager. Teenage resistant (rebellion) comes with the children becoming aware of the past demands and conflicts, and feeling that they were treated unfairly and are now reacting in a conscious stubborn way as a result.

Many parents ask at what age they should expect their children to clean up or to make their own bed. Most parents look at these simple chores as a chance to teach responsibility. So, why doesn't it go smoothly? The child at four or five is physically capable of helping to make a bed, just as she is physically capable of putting her toys away. She does not do either job consistently because they do not matter to her as it does to the mother. Developmentally, many four or five year olds cannot see any reason to do it. If they think about it at all, it is probably to wonder why we are putting the toys away when we will be getting them out again.

Once again the heart of the problem is that teaching responsibility comes too early. The situation changes into an issue of compliance as your expectations are not met. When we become angry and punitive, we have lost sight of what we really wanted to instill in our child. Compliance becomes more important than learning responsibility. For the young child it should be an experience of working together as part of the family.

The other aspect of this issue is that the parent feels they are teaching responsibility by giving a chore. Telling the child to do a task and returning later to see if it has been done is more a test than a teaching process. The parent has asked them to take responsibility, not taught them how to take it.

You can start the process at two or three if your mindset is not that your child better finish his chore or else. If you start like the Mongolian family and make it a join effort and naturally increase his role as the child becomes more capable, there is a better chance that the child will start to do the task.

Try this approach: Tell your three-year-old: "let's make your bed," and then you, the parent, do 95 percent of the work at first. Have a smile on your face and make it a nice time for both of you because you are doing something together. Do not have an attitude that communicates, "This isn't a big job and you'd better do it."

As time goes on your child does more, and finally he generally can do it by himself. Later, you might say that you will take care of it for him because you know he has other things he needs to do. Don't forget to include an occasional pillow fight! Not making it "his chore," will make it less likely to be an issue. It also promotes the sense of our doing things together as a family and helping each other. It may even be a pleasant memory of a pillow fight with mom.

When we start teaching responsibility in the area of chores, our expectations are crucial. Some parents say that they did start out in a positive way, but that when nothing was getting done, they had to resort to a harder line, and it was the same old story. They are convinced that the nice way does not work, but the real problem was expecting too much too early.

If the parents had been willing to accept whatever their children contributed, rather than having a preconceived goal of getting the job done no matter how long it takes and how young the child is, the child would feel good that he had helped. It is more likely that he will help willingly next time, especially if a little fun is mixed into the work.

Run for Fun

In one consultation I asked a father who loves to run if his ten-year-old son likes to run with him. The dad said that his son did at first, but now after even short runs he complains about wanting to stop. The father knows that he can do it and tries to push him to do more, but the child's motivation is different than his father's. The father's pushing at this stage could eventually lead to the child not wanting to run at all, because it has become contentious and there is a negative feeling in his interactions with his dad.

Just like chores, putting "fun" into more manageable segments allows the child to see that running is a good time with his dad. Stopping while the child is still having fun and asking him if he wants to do more is an approach that may work better than just urging him to do more because you know he can.

Does everything have to be fun? Of course not, but, if we ask our child for perfect participation and completion of his chores from day one, we will start him on a path of resistance to anything we ask him to do and resentment for punishments he experiences. Again, it may be that the terminology is not exact. Rather than being about "responsibility," it should be more about being willing to participate in helping the family. Later, as the child becomes older, it can become the basis for taking responsibility in all aspects of his life.

Responsibility in School

Think about being stage-setters and your children the actors who do the performing. Parents can do many things to make it possible for their children to performance well, but in the end, the children must be the ones who act. Take homework, for an example. Parents are often asked to check their children's work and make sure that it has been done correctly. They can easily become too involved in this situation.

In school, children face two general academic missions: First, is learning the lesson and doing it well. Second, and just as important, is learning how to learn. Without realizing it, parents often take the opportunity of "learning how to learn" away from their child. They may have the child do the initial work, but then take charge of checking the answers, the neatness, etc. so that the homework is perfect.

Learning to handle this latter task is important for the child's total education. She not only needs to learn to do the work, but also to take responsibility for it. Parents should be a resource for their child and they should monitor her progress, but the more they let their child take responsibility for her work, the more she will learn. She will have learned more than mere facts, she will have learned that she is capable of doing a job well. Remember how proud we were when we proclaimed, "I did it all by myself!"

Every year some freshmen in colleges that admit highly qualified students flunk out in the first semester. While there are many reasons for this, I'm sure that some are students whose parents took over the responsibility to get the work done. Now on their own, some students flounder because they did not learn to take the responsibility for themselves. There is no one there to make them study and get their work done, and they fail without their parents to check on and push them.

The real life lesson that parents are trying to pass on to their children is to take responsibility for themselves. It takes guidance from an understanding parent when the child is young. As the child matures, let her come to you when she feels the need for help. Your interventions are still needed to make sure that she is on track, but should more often be macro- not micro- in nature. Besides, do you really understand the "new math?"

The problem in this competitive world is that parents can be too eager to make sure that their child always gets her work done in a perfect way. Not only in school, but in other areas of your child's life you should encourage her to do things on her own even though she may fail. If her self-esteem is intact, she has resilience and she feels your support, she will try again and when she succeeds, she will have learned a lesson about hard work and not giving up, and her success will be all that much sweeter.

Balancing Responsibility

Improving the parent-child relationship positions us to help our children to grow and succeed. Raising our child in a more helpful, mentoring way rather than an adversarial way makes all the difference. Still, the challenge is to strike a balance between being helpful and nurturing, while not being overbearing and too controlling. The helicopter mom, aided and abetted by the cell phone, is starting to give way to a trend of giving more responsibility and self-reliance back to the child.

I think that this issue will swing back and forth from excess on one side to the other forever. It doesn't really matter, if the parents have enriched their children with self-esteem and the ability to take responsibility for themselves.

Summary

- At first, young children should participate in helping the family without the expectation that they will complete the task
- Enjoying working to their abilities with the family will lead to taking responsibilities in the adult sense
- Their abilities grow with them
- Parents are the stage-setters and the children the actors.
- Macro-manage school

EPILOGUE

Love is that condition in which the happiness of another   person is essential to your own.

- Robert A. Heinlein
  A Stranger in a Strange Land

I was being interviewed by a couple prior to the birth of their first child. Amy, the mother-to-be, had gone to school with our children, so we were having a casual and enjoyable conversation. Her husband asked, "Just exactly what was the scope of my interaction with them going to be?" I told him that I would care for the baby's medical needs, and at the well-child visits I would discuss with them how to raise a great child. Then he turned to Amy, and with a deadpan face asked, "You know his kids, how did they turn out?"

In the first few years of raising our children my wife and I used the techniques of Parenting 101. There were many confrontations and penalties for not complying and finishing chores. We were heavy into obedience and compliance as standards of parenting. We had battles over how they ate. We all had our share of angry looks. Underneath all of this we wished that there was a friendlier way to teach life's lessons to our children. We loved them dearly, but we were treating them as adversaries. We felt the pain of an adversarial relationship, but didn't think of its effect on our children.

One day it occurred to me that I couldn't remember ever being punished by my mother when I was growing up. I think that she probably did use some coercion, but never physical punishment or many angry words. I don't remember her words or actions, but I still remember how she made me feel; she made me feel good about myself. She always had fun with my brother and me. Somehow without reading a book about raising kids or going to college she understood how to raise us. She knew we were just immature kids. The few cross words we heard were usually mixed with a laugh or smile. Still, we both grew up well within the rules and have lead productive lives.

I have three cousins about ten years older than me who all remembered her as their Peter Pan when they were growing up. She was the one that they looked for when they needed help or wanted to have more fun than they were supposed to have. I believe that her secret was that she never demeaned us nor did anything to make any of us doubt her commitment to and love for us.

After discussing stopping our unpleasant encounters with our young children, my wife and I decided to try to curb our stern and harsh approach and try to be more pleasant in our encounters with our children. We still were strong in our beliefs of good behavior but began to find that firmness with a smile seemed to work better than the stern threatening pose. We started to take more responsibility to learn how to make things work better for everyone by being proactive in solving problems and teaching our children in a positive way. There was less demanding of "better behavior or else." This change in style of parenting seemed to feed on itself and it became natural to us to be more helpful and less critical. We were on a roll, we had established our new starting point.

Once positioned, over time we started to automatically try to find solutions that helped both us and them and we became good friendly resources for them. There were still issues that were not easily resolved, but I think that they came to know that we were trying to help them.   I think it is hard to put our path into a few words, it was not a lesson that came with a dramatic or memorable event where we could all look back and say, "Remember how we all used to be at each other's throats and then this event changed everything".

These good relationships were built over the years, day by day, in the everyday things that our children experienced. I think that we succeeded in demonstrating to them the fact that we love them, tried not to be judgmental, and always supported them no matter how wild and crazy their plans were. They knew that they would always get a fair hearing from their parents, and that the restrictions and limitations that we set were thought through and not arbitrary (usually).

Once (or maybe even twice) my children demanded that I do something because "you promised, Dad." My answer was that I knew I had not promised, because I never knew what might come up in my life as a doctor. Instead, I told them, they could always count on the fact that I would always do the best I could for them because I loved and cared about them so much.

I think that our children grew up in an atmosphere

where they knew how much we loved them, and, most importantly, this love for them was not obscured by a parenting style that used demands and threats of punishment and diminished their self-esteem. While neither they nor we were anywhere near perfect—we all made many mistakes along the way—we kept trying to make sure that they knew how much we loved them and cared about them. I think that the extent to which we succeeded was due to the fact that we became proactive. We quit the traditional crime-and-punishment method and learned how to mentor and teach them to become civil and productive people.

In sum, reaching our goal of having children who like themselves, who like us (and whom we like in return), and who like each other, required that my wife and I reflect on the flaws in past parenting theories and methods, Parenting 101. We needed to make a choice to work at becoming better parents by teaching, mentoring, and being proactive. We committed to nurturing, maintaining, and growing their self-esteem.

The first step is to recognize that it is your responsibility to make the relationship with your child friendly and helpful. Stop and think about this, it really is a pivotal point. You need to recognize their developmental limitations, and not put them in situations that are over their heads, especially when they are younger. When there is a problem, use your better judgment and abilities to help them resolve it, instead of demanding that they rise to the occasion.

In fact, remove terminology like "demand," "compliance," "pick my battles," "discipline" and other adversarial terms from the conversation. It can be harder to do than you might think, because we have become accustomed to the old rather demeaning vocabulary that past generations have used to communicate with their children. Changing the terminology we use with and about our children, being helpful rather than demanding, infuses your relationship with good will. It starts out our interactions in a positive way. It makes our child comfortable approaching us with a problem knowing we will help them to solve it, not get mad or upset at their shortcomings.

Good and well-intentioned new parents still must study and learn to become great parents. It is difficult to change age-old patterns and ways of being, especially when we feel that we turned out alright under the old, authoritarian methods of our parents. That is not proof that those methods worked, but proof that love conquers all, and that we have selective memories.

The love of parents for their children is what comforts children even when their parents are acting less than perfectly. The overwhelming love of the parent for his or her child is a powerful antidote for all the mistakes that they make.

A good sense of humor is also an important part of the parent's interface with his children. I have seen parents seriously angry over the most trivial matters. I suspect that it was because while the issue may have been trivial, the lack of compliance was treated as an act of defiance that must be dealt with in a strong way to prevent future problems. Not worrying about compliance and instead thinking of a friendlier way to move the problem along often gets the job done better. Your smile and good humor signal to your child that he can discuss his problems with the expectation that he will get help and sympathy.

Rather than following a traditional pattern of harsh and demanding parenting, wouldn't it be wonderful to enjoy the whole process of raising a caring and productive child, while also being a great resource and friend to your children all through their lives?

There will be other people in your children's lives who will have special relationships with them, but if you have a great journey with your children while you raise them, no relationship will be more special than yours.

APPENDIX: SPECIAL CASES

This appendix covers areas that fall within the overall picture of what has been discussed in this book, but are placed separately in this section for emphasis and easier access because of the importance of and the frequency that these issues were brought up and discussed.

Water Safety

Water safety was something that I spent time on at every well child visit until all the children in a family were truly water safe. The reason is simple. A drowning is the most horrific preventable accident. It affects everyone in the family with overwhelming guilty and changes lives forever.

Here is what I tell parents to do in a proactive way to safeguard their children around water:

- One adult and only one should be responsible for one and only one non-swimmer when they are near water, including the swimming pool, hot tub/sauna, lake, river, or ocean. In a crisis with one child, a second will be forgotten.

- Be absolutely clear on which person is responsible for the child. If "everyone (parents and grandparents) is watching", after a while no one really is because each person assumes the other is paying attention. This is especially true if the mother steps away.

- The non-swimmer should not be your top priority; he should be your only priority. You should not be working on something nearby at the same time or reading as you "watch." Even conversations can distract you.

- Your child's love or fear of water is not a factor. The child who is afraid of water is just as likely to fall in if we are not watchful.

- Teenagers and older siblings should not be asked to watch non-swimmers. A mishap can ruin their lives forever. Teenagers are not always 100 percent attentive. There is a reason their car insurance is more expensive than that of adults. Cell phones and texting have increased their level of distraction as well.

- Drown-proofing lessons for toddlers and babies are worthless. The notion that a baby or toddler will save themselves because of these lessons is ludicrous. They can even lead to a false sense of security. The first two near-drownings that I was involved with were "so called drown-proofed toddlers in unsecured family pools The AAP does not recommend them before age three or four.

- All safety equipment (covers, fences, alarms, etc.) must be foolproof.

I have been involved with or heard of children drowning

when any of these guidelines has been ignored. I have personally rescued two toddlers floating face down in a baby pool bobbing in the water next to their mothers who were chatting with their friends

A mother confessed that she learned what one-on-one responsibility meant when she lost track of her three-year-old during a beach lunch in Hawaii. She finally spotted her fifty yards away walking in the surf. All the adults looked at each other and said, "I thought you were watching her." No one really took responsibility because they were "all watching her." One mother I know went so far as to make a banner that read, "I'm responsible for the baby," and made whoever was in charge carry it while she or he was watching.

Most parents have been very receptive of these rules and have implemented them strictly, by their report. The danger is so clear and horrifying that the parents clearly see that the safety of their child is 100 percent their responsibility.

Eating Properly

There is more written about food and proper eating than any other subject. Every year there are best-selling books on dieting, sugar laden foods, organic or properly raised veggies and meat, healthier foods, and holier-than-thou foods. These books are often informative and worthwhile, but they often distract the reader from the issue of eating a wide variety of foods and the appropriate number of calories.

For example, when I asked an open-ended question such as, does your child eat well? The answers spanned a wide range and often helped to reveal the parent's perception of what was most important in feeding her child. The answers often included: "he eats a lot (number one answer), I don't give any junk food; we don't eat any sugary foods; we eat mostly organic; or I make all her food." Is there anything wrong with these responses? No, but they are not addressing the first two points of eating properly: eating the appropriate number of calories and eating a variety of foods.

"He eats a lot" comes up the most when the child is five-years-old or younger. Why is this so prevalent? I think that it comes from a concern based on a false observation; the child is not eating enough. When the child is a toddler they are usually eating enough calories, but generally eating less food than the parent expects. I will discuss this more later. For now, let's move on to the next answer. The quality and type of the food has become increasingly important. Not giving junk or fast food is definitely a good idea, but is it the main issue in poor eating? This is one impasse that the parent is unlikely to win. Many parents have recounted their own tales of being made to sit at the table for hours, or holding food in their mouth and never swallowing it.

Remember, we want him to eat a wide variety of food, and the appropriate number of calories, and do it intuitively. What has happened to make this impasse such a common complaint?

Let Us Go Back to the Beginning

Eating properly entails three things:

- Consuming the appropriate number of calories.
- Eating a wide variety of foods that encompass all essential nutrients.

- And, most importantly, doing it intuitively.

So, why can feeding a child be so difficult? Mostly, it has to do with misinformation, miscalculations, and misperceptions. have I missed anything?

Feeding your fetus is about as intuitive as it gets. You need to feed yourself well and avoid alcohol, smoking, moldy cheese, and medications that could affect your developing baby. Your newborn is also fed pretty intuitively once you have established breast-feeding. While you are aware of when you want to feed the baby and may manipulate the frequency and feeding, even when you think that the feeding was short, you accept it and go to the next time. A mother has no idea of how much she gave at a given breast-feeding, but generally doesn't try to manipulate the situation.

At six months pediatricians advise starting solids, and often a bottle is used to give the milk. Common enough, many do this. So what is the problem? We think, therefore, we are … in trouble. We often over-think and under-think the issue at the same time. That is, once we can see what we are doing, we want to know exactly how much to give and when to give it. These are reasonable questions that do not have definite answers. But, most of us (including me) are unlikely to look up the number of calories that our child needs at their weight, much less learn to count the calories in their food. Fortunately, at this age, and up to one year plus, we do tend to get it right.

I noticed that my parents were generally happy with the way their children ate up to age one, and unhappy with their "picky" two-year-old. They were unhappy but resigned to it. After all, didn't all her friends have the same problem? Even some of the books reinforced this as a "normal phase." I have to admit that I also accepted it early on, but as I began to question the terrible twos as a normal phase, it also seemed not so natural that a child who ate widely as a one-year-old should become "naturally picky" as a two-year-old.

What makes analyzing the issue so difficult is that we automatically blame conflicts with our children on them. Parenting folklore is replete with phrases like "the picky" toddler, the "terrible twos," "teenage rebellion," and many others. These issues could be the subject of a entire book themselves, but suffice it to say here that the adult is blaming these problems on the child, and the child cannot put up an effective rebuttal. But when he tries, he is characterized with negative stereotypes of being difficult, stubborn, etc. Unfortunately, this feeling and conclusion is often reinforced by grandparents and friends who had the same problems before you.

Self-examination is difficult when we are trying to determine who needs to change their ways in a conflict. It is even harder to find fault with oneself when you are dealing with your child. After all, we are supposed to be in charge. If we can put aside this way of thinking, we can explore the question more fully.

What Are the Factors That Have Led to the Picky Eater?

First, the form of the food has changed. It was a semi-liquid, and not something that we ate with them. Thus we could not directly compare them with how much we were eating. When the child starts eating table food, that is, the same type of food that we are eating, we have a ready reference to judge how they are eating compared to a known standard, ourselves. Now we are realistic enough not to expect them to eat as much as ourselves, but how much should they eat in comparison? Half as much, or two thirds?

Rather than actually finding out what they should eat and how much food that actually is, we tend to guess, and then expect them to eat all of what we have casually estimated. Often we do not consider that they are drinking a substantial amount of calories in the form of milk, while our own drinks are often devoid of calories. Thus our estimates tend to be even more flawed. This leads to what I believe is the fundamental problem in our feeding plan.

We offer too much food and expect the child to eat everything we have placed before them. This is in spite of the fact that we usually have not calculated the calories in their food, nor do we have any idea how many calories would be appropriate to offer at the given meal. But do we need to do these calculations? No, not if we trust that the child will intuitively eat as much as his hunger tells him to eat.

Thus, if we place a plate before the child with four different foods on it, and check the plate after he is done, we may see that:

- He has eaten it all and wants more
- He has eaten all the food and does not want anymore
- He eats half the food and says he is done

In the first case, we have guessed and offered him less than he wanted (which hardly ever happens). In the second case, we have guessed and are right on target as to his caloric needs (do we still offer more?)

The third case is the most typical. We have guessed way

too much and as a consequence, he has stopped after eating half the food offered. This would be okay if he ate half of each item we offered him. But, what would you do if you were offered larger than necessary portions of four foods, two of which you loved, and two which you didn't care as much for? Wouldn't your tendency be to eat your favorites first? And if you had twice as many calories on your plate as you needed to satisfy your hunger, isn't it likely that you would eat your favorites first, and not feel hungry enough to eat much of or any of the foods that you were not crazy about, since the large portions allowed you to satisfy your hunger while only eating your favorites?

This is what happens to our one-and-a-half year old. We place a plate before him that has portions that are twice the calories that he needs. He eats his two favorites first, gets full, and does not eat the remaining two piles. Instead of recognizing that they have offered way too much food, most parents feel that he only ate half as much food as he should have and that he does not like the two foods that he has not touched. It usually does not cross the parent's mind that they might have offered too much food. In fact, many parents will offer more of what he liked and ate, thus reinforcing their child's shunning of those foods that were just okay. Soon he will have been inadvertently taught that he no longer has to eat those marginal foods

Then begin the strategies to entice or force the child to eat what they have left on the plate. Usually it starts as a sense of duty to get the child to eat in a healthy way. Soon, it becomes less about food and nutrition, and more about authority, compliance, and, ultimately, discipline. Have you heard of friends (or yourself) sitting alone at the table for an hour until something (usually green and healthy) was eaten, or, more likely, a privilege is finally taken away?

A father told me that his daughter did eat everything, but

he had to sit and coax her for almost an hour every night. What a kind and patient father. I asked, "Do you enjoy doing this?" He said no, but that is what it takes to get her to eat anything. I suggested that he try to limit meals to fifteen minutes, and see what happened. He came back a few weeks later and reported that after a few times of having her plate whisked away before she was done, she had started finishing in the allotted time. .The parent is often an instigator and enabler in eating problems.

Other observations:

- Restaurants offer a kids menu that reflect what they know your child is likely to eat. Chicken fingers, cheese pizza, spaghetti, and grilled cheese are there. Oh, I almost forgot, "Do you want fries with it?" I encourage parents to reject the kid's menu and just share their own oversized portion with their toddlers. It gives better quality food and variety to the child.
- "No kid would eat that!" is often heard when an ethnic food is offered. But there are millions of little kids eating Indian and Chinese food every day. It is what is available to eat, so they eat it. Many of the foods in question are not that exotic, just ones that the parent turned their noses up to themselves.

The plan for making sure your child eats properly. It is important to start the plan when you start solids, and to believe that the child will stop when he is no longer hunger:

- Offer four equal portions of food.
- If food is left on the plate after the meal, assume you

have offered too much. Generally, what they like best will be finished and the less liked left.

- But, at the next meal, offer the four portions equally cut back. If there is still food left on the plate, continue to cut the portions back equally, until the offered plate is usually completely finished. This is how much food the child needs.

- Be sure to rotate your child's menu to be as varied as yours. If you are picky, remember it was your mother's fault, but try to eat better too.

Like most paradigm-changing advice, I have found that many parents find it hard to change their behavior. You have to take that first step, now. Just as when a person goes on a diet, it's about committing and going for it. Those who have, report that their children eat as well as they do, and are the envy of their fellow parents, who are amazed that it did not take force.

RECOMMENDED READING

Loving Your Child Is Not Enough: Positive Discipline That Works
  Nancy Samalin
  Penguin Books

Summerhill
  A.S. Neill
  Wallaby Books

Children Learn What They Live
  Dorothy Law Nolte and Rachel Harris
  Workman Publishing

1 -2 – 3 MAGIC
  THOMAS w. Phelan, PhD
  Sourcebooks

How To Raise An Adult
  Julie Lythcott-Harris
  Henry Holt and Co. LLC

Nurture Shock
  Po Bronson and Ashley Merryman
  Hachette

Peaceful Parent, Happy Kids
  Dr. Laura Markham
  Perigee book

What Great Parents Do
  Erica Reischer, PhD
  TascherPerigee

Bring Up BeBe
  Pamela Druckerman
  Penguin Books

Big History
  Cynthia Stokes Brown
  The New Press

CPSIA information can be obtained
at www.ICGtesting.com
Printed in the USA
LVHW03s1657290618
582295LV00014B/177/P